The Litera

Po

The Literary Agenda

Poetry

DAVID CONSTANTINE

OXFORD
UNIVERSITY PRESS

OXFORD
UNIVERSITY PRESS

Great Clarendon Street, Oxford, OX2 6DP,
United Kingdom

Oxford University Press is a department of the University of Oxford.
It furthers the University's objective of excellence in research, scholarship,
and education by publishing worldwide. Oxford is a registered trade mark of
Oxford University Press in the UK and in certain other countries

First Edition published in 2013

Impression: 1

British Library Cataloguing in Publication Data

Data available

ISBN 978-0-19-969847-9

Printed in Great Britain by
Clays Ltd, St Ives plc

Series Introduction

The Crisis in, the Threat to, the Plight of the Humanities: enter these phrases in Google's search engine and there are 23 million results, in a great fifty-year-long cry of distress, outrage, fear, and melancholy. Grant, even, that every single anxiety and complaint in that catalogue of woe is fully justified—the lack of public support for the arts, the cutbacks in government funding for the humanities, the imminent transformation of a literary and verbal culture by visual/virtual/digital media, the decline of reading...And still, though it were all true, and just because it might be, there would remain the problem of the response itself. Too often there's recourse to the shrill moan of offended piety or a defeatist withdrawal into professionalism.

The Literary Agenda is a series of short polemical monographs that believes there is a great deal that needs to be said about the state of literary education inside schools and universities and more fundamentally about the importance of literature and of reading in the wider world. The category of 'the literary' has always been contentious. What *is* clear, however, is how increasingly it is dismissed or is unrecognized as a way of thinking or an arena for thought. It is sceptically challenged from within, for example, by the sometimes rival claims of cultural history, contextualized explanation, or media studies. It is shaken from without by even greater pressures: by economic exigency and the severe social attitudes that can follow from it; by technological change that may leave the traditional forms of serious human communication looking merely antiquated. For just these reasons this is the right time for renewal, to start reinvigorated work into the meaning and value of literary reading for the sake of the future.

It is certainly no time to retreat within institutional walls. For all the academic resistance to 'instrumentalism', to governmental measurements of public impact and practical utility, literature exists in and across society. The 'literary' is not pure or specialized or self-confined; it is not restricted to the practitioner in writing or the academic in studying. It exists in the whole range of the world which is its subject matter: it consists in what non-writers actively receive from writings when, for example, they start to see the world more imaginatively as a result of reading novels and begin to think more carefully about human personality. It comes from literature making available much of human life that would not otherwise be existent to thought or recognizable as knowledge. If it is true that involvement in literature, so far from being a minority aesthetic, represents a significant contribution to the life of human thought, then that idea has to be argued at the public level without succumbing to a hollow rhetoric or bowing to a reductive world-view. Hence the effort of this series to take its place *between* literature and the world. The double-sided commitment to occupying that place and establishing its reality is the only 'agenda' here, without further prescription as to what should then be thought or done within it.

What is at stake is not simply some defensive or apologetic 'justification' in the abstract. The case as to why literature matters in the world not only has to be argued conceptually and strongly tested by thought, it should be given presence, performed, and brought to life in the way that literature itself does. That is why this series includes the writers themselves, the novelists and poets, in order to try to close the gap between the thinking of the artists and the thinking of those who read and study them. It is why it also involves other kinds of thinkers—the philosopher, the theologian, the psychologist, the neuroscientist—examining the role of literature within their own life's work and thought, and the effect of that work, in turn, upon literary thinking. This series admits and encourages personal voices in an unpredictable variety of individual approach and expression, speaking wherever possible across countries and disciplines and temperaments. It aims for something more than intellectual assent: rather the literary sense of what it is like to feel the thought, to embody an idea in a person, to bring it to being in a narrative or in aid of adventurous reflection. If the artists refer to their own works, if other thinkers return to ideas that have marked much of their working life, that is not their vanity nor a failure of originality. It is what the series has asked of them: to speak out of what they know and care about, in whatever language can best serve their most serious thinking, and without the necessity of trying to cover every issue or meet every objection in each volume.

Philip Davis

Acknowledgements

Unless otherwise indicated, the translations in this monograph are my own.

My thanks are due to the following publishers and copyright-holders for permission to reprint or quote from the poems and prose works included in this monograph: Bertolt Brecht: 'Schlechte Zeit für Lyrik' (© Bertolt-Brecht-Erben / Suhrkamp Verlag), in my translation; Robert Graves: 'The Cool Web' (in *Collected Poems*, vol. 1, Carcanet Press, 1995; and for the electronic rights, A. P. Watt); Derek Mahon, 'Tractatus' from *New Collected Poems* (2012) by kind permission of the author and The Gallery Press <http://www.gallerypress.com>; Harry Martinson: 'Cable-Ship', translated by Robin Fulton (in *Chickweed Wintergreen*, Bloodaxe Books, 2010); Miklós Radnóti: 'Letter to my Wife' (*Modern Poetry in Translation*, and the translator Stephen Capus); Edward Thomas, 'The sun used to shine' (in *The Annotated Collected Poems*, Bloodaxe Books, 2008); R. S. Thomas: 'In Church' (in *Selected Poems*, Bloodaxe Books, 1986); Jeanette Winterson extract from *Why Be Happy When You Can Be Normal?* by Jeanette Winterson, reproduced by kind permission of Peters Fraser & Dunlop <http://www.petersfraser-dunlop.com>, published by Jonathan Cape, reprinted by permission of The Random House Group Limited; Robert Frost, 'Iris by Night' from *The Poetry of Robert Frost*, ed. Edward Connery Latham, published by Jonathan Cape, reprinted by permission of The Random House Group Limited; Philip Larkin, 'Wedding-Wind', from *Collected Poems*, reprinted by permission of Faber and Faber.

Contents

Introduction

Note

The grounds for this monograph lie in my own experience of reading and trying to write poetry, which experience is inevitably partial. I was born in 1944, studied Modern Languages, taught German language and literature, and feel myself to be both very English and very European. I am a translator, chiefly out of German. Most of my living and travelling 'abroad' has been in Europe and to a large extent I have developed my social and political concerns and allegiances in dealings with the history and the present circumstances of Britain in Europe. This life has necessarily shaped my understanding of poetry, what I ask of it, and what kinds of poetry I like and don't like. I have always read beyond Europe, especially in my nine years as co-editor of *Modern Poetry in Translation*, a magazine whose constituency is the International Republic of Letters. Still my knowledge is partial. Poetry itself, however, is abundant and comprehensively various; and I can hope to say things about it, out of my own experience, that readers will answer out of theirs. 'Where there is much desire to learn, there of necessity will be much arguing, much writing, many opinions; for opinions in good men is but knowledge in the making': those words from Milton's *Areopagitica* hung framed on the wall in my English teacher's classroom. They come back to me now—particularly 'knowledge in the making'—as very apt for an attempt to engage people in thinking about and, more still, in reading poetry.

Remembering that teacher, two or three others also come to mind, at school and at university, also several fellow-pupils and fellow-students and students of my own who confirmed me in my love of poetry and helped me greatly in my understanding of it. Even with those of them who are dead, my conversation continues, I recall their words, their tones of voice, can imagine how they might answer if I put new questions to them, I have books of poetry on my shelves that they gave me or recommended to me. So it continues, letter and spirit.

For this particular writing I am most indebted to Helen Constantine, who read it all and discussed it with me; to Sasha Dugdale, for 'much arguing' over its grounds; and to Phil Davis, who, as editor and friend, always encouraging, patiently helped me to shape it better. I thank Tom Chandler for his patient, meticulous, and tactful copyediting, and Simon Constantine for helping me with the Index.

Poetry, society, and the state

My premise is: literature matters. It matters for individuals and for the society they are members of. We live now in a time and a place where that premise is inadequately or only nominally acknowledged, or is flatly denied. Humane letters are sliding (being shoved) towards the margins; out there, marginal, peripheral, they cannot thrive. Therefore we have to answer back, and not in any personal interest but for the public good. I shall deal chiefly with poetry, the writing and the reading of it, but some of what I say might apply to other literary genres also. I don't think poetry a grace or a luxury that society might adorn itself with from time to time and drop altogether when it pleases. And I don't think that poetry is for the few, happy or not. It is for the many, belongs and can only thrive among them, speaks of and to their concerns. No society that I know of has done without poetry; some have striven officiously to exterminate it and failed; which must mean that its will to live is very great and that we need it.

Poetry in society. Poetry gets written, for the most part, in solitude or in the sort of concentration that temporarily isolates the poet from society; often it is read in such a solitude and isolating concentration also. But writer and reader in their kindred activities never cease being social creatures and the poetry they write or read is thoroughly informed by the society they live in. That is a fact and not in the least a matter of regret. I don't mean that poetry is in any essential way restricted by or to the particular society in which it is written or read; only that it is a thoroughly social activity and its social nature constitutes a large part of its value.

Poetry and the state. By 'the state' I mean the organization and governance of society which will be shaped by the dominant politics and will at any one time in any one place be more or less likely to nurture or stunt the citizens so organized and governed. The relationship of poetry with the social order has never been easy and since Romanticism it has been decidedly and unavoidably fraught.

Society and the state may (but need not) in practice amount to the same thing. A people shaped and indoctrinated by a particular social order may not be able to distinguish itself from and act or think independently of the dominant politics and its structures by which they are organized and governed. A particular ideology—that of the market, for example—may be so successfully instilled into so large a proportion of the people that it will come to seem not just the normal but also the only way of being human. A society in that mindset will have very little time for poetry. Or, put the other way, in such a society the writing and reading of poetry will perforce be a contrary act, an act of opposition. Then by its very nature affirming a way of being human that the social order disregards, despises, or denies, poetry may seem to be a marginal and forlorn activity and consequently negligible; and some poets have wilfully furthered that marginalization, so courting their own extinction. A large part of my endeavour will consist in trying to persuade any who need persuading that poetry springs from and belongs in the heart of society and that it does good there.

Common and strange. Poetry is at one and the same time plumb in the midst of social living and at an angle to it, odd, slant, strange. It is common, commonplace, it thrives in and serves our common lives, but does so by virtue of its slant relationship to them. Poetry lives in that dynamic tension; fails and dies without it. The material of poetry is the stuff of common life, the lives real people live and might live in the here and now; its medium is words, which are the common property of the tribe, at everyone's disposal; and out of those common words it makes art, using words strangely, and so works estrangingly, which is to say illuminatingly and unsettlingly, on the common life to which we have become habituated.

Robert Graves (in his poem 'From the Embassy') calls the poet 'an ambassador of Otherwhere'. The currency of that land, its language, is 'Otherwhereish'. Made of our common words, poetry sounds, in the company of those words, like speech brought to us by translation from abroad. Poetry signals its strangeness. Formerly it did so by the use of metre, rhyme, particular forms and arrangements of the lines, a diction very different from that of common speech. These were the markers of its otherness. They said to the reader or listener: this is poetry, a particular kind and degree of attention is being asked of you; the pleasure and the benefits are great, but to come into them you have to attend otherwise than you attend to any other kind of language. 'Metre,' says Coleridge in his *Biographia Literaria*, 'in itself is simply a stimulant of the attention, and therefore excites the question: Why is the attention to be thus stimulated?' And his answer to that question is: 'I write in metre, because I am about to use a language different from that of prose.'[1] Metre is a sign that what you are reading or listening to is poetry. So alerted, you read and listen in a way that is consonant with that language.

Many of the abovementioned markers have fallen away in much recent and contemporary English verse; the fear being, I suppose, that far from awakening attention to something vital and always new they will sound like reminders of something as out of place in modern society as quill pens and inkwells—at best quaint, like the fancy dress and bizarre courtesies in the House of Lords, at worst wholly irrelevant and negligible. Wordsworth himself—whom Coleridge in the *Biographia* has constantly in mind—quite programmatically sought to establish the *lingua communis*, 'the real language of men',[2] as the proper language of poetry. Coleridge's objections to that programme spring from his fear that by wholly adopting such a language poetry would lose its purchase on the reader's life. And if poets shifting exclusively into that register also let go the other markers of poetry's distinctiveness (a possibility which Wordsworth never entertained) they risk failure in the whole poetic undertaking, which is to command attention for an experience which, so poets believe, people and the society they live in cannot, and should not try to, do without. In practice, the poets who don't employ rhyme, metre, and stanzaic forms and who keep close to common speech, must devise other ways and means of quickening the faculty latent in everyone for the good that poetry brings. Some external markers of otherness are necessary or the poem will not command attention and will not be able to bear upon the quotidian reality in which poet and reader live their lives.

Notes

1. Samuel Taylor Coleridge, *Biographia Literaria* (London: J. M. Dent, 1949), 182. All further references to this—the Everyman edition—of *Biographia Literaria* are included as *BL* and page number in my text.
2. William Wordsworth, 'Preface to the Lyrical Ballads', in *The Poetical Works of Wordsworth*, ed. Thomas Hutchinson (Oxford: Clarendon Press, 1959), 734.

1

The Writing and Reading of Poetry

Realization

Writing and reading are kindred acts. In both a realization takes place. Both are 'knowledge in the making'. For most poets on most occasions writing is the slow process by which the idea of the poem is realized. By 'idea' I mean the whole complex of thoughts, images, feelings, memories, and imaginings that on each occasion go into the making of the particular poem.

It is true that sometimes a poet may simply write out a poem as though under dictation or as though seeing it and reading it from a script already completed in the head. Goethe relates that as a young man he would rise in the night under compulsion like a sleepwalker and write out a finished poem slant across—in too much haste to straighten—the first sheet of paper to hand. And for this writing he preferred pencil, because that was softer, to a quill pen which by its scratching might wake him out of his trance.[1] Similarly, in 1797, approaching fifty, he wrote out a couple of his most celebrated ballads as though from a finished text, but acknowledged that he had carried them in him, gestating, for fifteen or twenty years. As a young man or in middle age Goethe's making of those poems was, whether rapid or very slow, a process of realization. It had gone on for hours or years with no, or only intermittent, conscious participation in it by the writer.

Most poetic composition, proceeding 'externally' on paper or on a screen, is messier, more obviously a struggle towards adequate realization. And always, in my own experience and in my understanding of other writers' accounts, it is only in the process of composition that the poet begins to realize what exactly the demands of the poem will turn out to be. Only by that process do you begin to

realize (in the sense of 'understand') what it is you are trying to real-
ize (in the sense of 'say', 'make palpable'). The idea of the poem is
realized in the process of composition: it is made real, present, and
palpable to the poet and so, later, to any willing reader. The means
of this realization is words: not just in their manifold meanings but
also in their order, their sounds, the shape they are given on the
page, their organization into lines and larger units. It would be true
to say that a poem achieves its realization in the entirety of its
rhythm, whether engendered by and against a strict prosody or in
some other discipline, the material living body of that rhythm being,
of course, words.

The idea of the poem has to be realized, for the poet's own
satisfaction, and also for its communication to other people. The
poem, not there even to the poet until its realization in a particu-
lar rhythm, is still only latently there when it appears in print on
a page. The reader is a vital participant in the making of the
poem. It is the reader who animates the conventional black signs
on a white page which we call the text. This act of enlivening
realization is not the same as but is kindred to the poet's own. It
is a steeping of oneself into the living text, a thorough and pleas-
urable engagement. The reader bodies the poem forth by bring-
ing to it (ideally) the sum total of her or his experience to date.
Focused by the grammar of the poem, by the real lexical senses
of the words in that particular order, reading closely with precise
attention, the reader necessarily and very beneficially converts the
poem into his or her own life—and enlarges that life in so doing.
Coleridge's term for this experience is 'pleasurable excitement'
(*BL*, 154, 180), as the words in their rhythm come to life in the
listener or reader.

Realization—making real and, as part of that, having things dawn
on you as you write or read—is a fair word to describe a good deal
of what goes on in the writing and reading of a poem.

A local habitation

'And as imagination bodies forth / The forms of things unknown,
the poet's pen / Turns them to shapes, and gives to airy nothing /
A local habitation and a name' (*A Midsummer Night's Dream*, 5.1,

14–17).[2] So says Theseus, not himself inclined to give much credence to the products of the 'seething brains' of lunatics, lovers, and poets. His loss. In the case of poetry, at least, he will deny himself the good effects of workings he has very well understood.

Writing a poem, as I said earlier, is a process of realizing as much as possible of the complex and immaterial matrix which constitutes its pre-existence. That matrix is the 'things unknown', which can't be known until they are bodied forth in forms, turned to shapes by the working imagination. The 'airy nothing' only becomes something—something real to the writer and to the subsequent readers—when by the act of writing it is given 'a local habitation and a name'.

In Bertolt Brecht's workroom, in the house friends lent him during his exile in Svendborg, stood the sentence, deriving through Lenin from Hegel: 'Die Wahrheit ist konkret' [truth is concrete]. Brecht's lover, Margarete Steffin, cut the letters out of cardboard, painted them black and stuck them to a beam, where he would see them. It was a reminder or admonishment against which he would measure his writing—all his writing: dramatic, theoretical, fiction, poetry. He looked up at it and asked himself: Have I realized the truth concretely enough? As a dramatist his chief interest was to externalize on stage the elements of the—most often contradictory and conflictual—situations his characters were in. Thus his Shen Te, 'the good woman of Sezuan', *demonstrates* her predicament by standing before the audience with, in one hand, the lease of her shop, which she must retain, to do good, and in the other a bill, which she cannot afford to pay. To survive as a charitable person, she invents and repeatedly inhabits her ruthless cousin Shui Ta, and in that persona, and pregnant by her exploitative lover, Sun, she becomes in herself (to use Brecht's own term) the bodily *Gestus* of the contradictions of her situation.[3]

Brecht's lyric poetry works similarly. He employs concrete instances, and even shapes his lines so that in their rhythm and where they break, they reinforce, point up or actually enact their sense. Like Shen Te, they are the *Gestus* of the situation Brecht wishes us to consider. Here is a poem he wrote in Svendborg in the late 1930s. 'The house painter' is his contemptuous name for Hitler.

Bad times for lyric poetry

But I know: only the happy
Are beloved. Their voices
Are heard with pleasure. Their faces are beautiful.

The crippled tree in the yard
Points to poor ground but
Passers-by call it a cripple
And rightly.

The green boats and the cheerful sails in the sound
I do not see. All I see is
The torn nets of the fishermen.
Why is my only speech
That the cottager's wife goes bowed and bent at forty?
The girls' breasts
Are as warm as they ever were.

In any poem of mine
A rhyme would seem almost a presumption.

In me quarrel
Joyous excitement at the apple tree in bloom
And horror at the house painter's speeches.
But only the latter
Drives me to my desk.

In practice, Brecht's poem (quite deliberately, I should say) contradicts the statement of restriction. He *does* see 'the green boats and the cheerful sails in the sound', they and the girls' warm breasts are as present in his poem as the things he thinks it his responsibility to treat. Hitler drives him to his desk; but in that compulsion lies also the love of a life that Hitler's victory would reduce or annihilate.

The Swedish poet Harry Martinson is as adept as Brecht at presenting a topic in telling concrete details. Thus here in his 'Cableship', translated by Robin Fulton:

We fished up the Atlantic cable between Barbados and Tortuga,
held up our lanterns
and patched over the gash on its back,
fifteen degrees north and sixty-one west.
When we put our ears to the gnawed part
we heard the murmuring in the cable.

> One of us said: 'It's the millionaires in Montreal and St John's
> discussing the price of Cuban sugar
> and the lowering of our wages.'

> We stood there long, thinking, in a lantern circle,
> we patient cable-fishers,
> then lowered the mended cable
> back to its place in the sea.

They bring the cable to light, they lift it into the light of the lanterns. So a truth is realized (in the cable) that they know already and that we perhaps need to learn.

As a materialist not much interested in (scarcely believing in) 'psychology', Brecht treated subjects whose components were social and therefore, in his view, always able to be concretely externalized. But any poet, materialist and politically engaged or not, would do well, in writing, to have 'truth is concrete' somewhere on view in the workroom or at least in mind. Working at a poem you are trying to make an adequate *Gestus* of all that the particular project entails; to induce an 'airy nothing' to materialize. The truth, however contradictory, many-faceted, fine and shifting it may be, must manifest itself concretely.

Periodically poetry has allowed itself to seem a mode apart in which rigour, common sense, and intelligence may, or even must, be abandoned in favour of vagueness, sentiment, and feeble-mindedness. 'Poetic' then comes to mean lax; as though in poetry, writing or reading it, you need not trouble to be as exact as you would have to be in other kinds of discourse. This shows itself in woolly and incoherent thinking, sloppy syntax, and in expressions that fall apart under close scrutiny. In his 1964 Oxford lectures Robert Graves worked his way through Quiller-Couch's *Oxford Book of English Verse* showing various well-loved items to be very laxly put together. He prefaced the exercise by telling his audience that in the anthology he found 'the standards of verse-craftsmanship...deplorably low, compared with those demanded from you undergraduates in, say, mathematics, physics and biology'. Then he performed exploratory surgery on Gray's 'On a favourite cat, drowned in a tub of gold fishes', 'Herrick's 'Gather ye rosebuds...', Keats's 'In a drear-nighted December', and much besides.[4] There was some idle mischief in all this but the underlying precept that poetry should be at least as careful in its composition as good prose, seemed to me then and still to be entirely sound. It does not mean that poetic language may not depart from strict conventional usage—often indeed it must—but such departures should be for good reason, for a provable effect in the writer's own voice and under a discipline of his or her own devising.

Rilke's fictional alter ego, Malte Laurids Brigge, recalls, as an iconic instance, that Félix Arvers with his dying breath corrected a nurse's mispronunciation of the word 'corridor'. He (Malte/Rilke) says of Arvers: 'Er war ein Dichter und hasste das Ungefähre' [he was a poet and detested approximations]. Then, reflecting further, he adds: 'or perhaps he was just concerned for the truth; or distressed that his last impression should be of a world continuing so sloppily. We shall never know. But we shouldn't think he was being pedantic.'[5]

At Christ's Hospital Coleridge's Classics teacher was the 'very sensible' and 'very severe' Reverend James Bowyer. 'I learned from him,' he says, 'that poetry, even that of the loftiest and, seemingly, that of the wildest odes, had a logic of its own, as severe as that of science; and more difficult, because more subtle, more complex, and dependent on more and more fugitive causes' (*BL*, 3).

Poetry is an exact discipline. The truth needs saying not just concretely but also in a language that is finely and exactly adequate; a language that will withstand close and critical scrutiny.

The reading of poetry should be likewise rigorous and exact. If in an inflecting language like Latin or German a noun appears in the genitive case, you can't read it as though it were in the accusative. If you don't know the lexical sense of a word, you look it up. You don't just guess or 'feel' it. Same with literary or cultural allusions: if you can't locate them or make sense of them by the context, ask, search, consult till you can. Intelligence should not be left on the doorstep when you enter a poem. You will need it. You can't just feel, intuit, guess your way through. The intelligence is not a *suspect* faculty. It is certainly not the binary opposite of feeling. It is quite possible to feel intelligently (or stupidly) and to think feelingly. The intelligence is the sixth sense, not separate from but pervaded by the other five. Poetry is an exact activity, it requires our keen attention. We don't have to be learned, nor will it help to be good at splitting hairs. But we do have to *attend exactly* to what is there. Again, reading should fit the thing being read. Poetry asks for all the faculties to be in play, as finely, intelligently, and feelingly as possible.

Exactness, saying as truly as you can what you mean and demanding to be read with a matching exactness, is a necessary virtue in poetry. And because poems are made of words and words are everybody's to use as they like, the exact use of them in poems becomes intrinsically a counter-attack against bad linguistic usage wherever it occurs. All the arts are an intrinsic answering back; but in the case of poetry, made of words and operating in a context of much public bad language (mendacious, evasive, slovenly, bureaucratic, ugly), the opposition is very obvious. Poetry is not a school of language; it is not poetry's job to purify the language of the tribe; but by being itself, doing what it does, it must often excite in us the wish not just to be more serious but also to be more exact. Seeing and saying exactly are a means of self-defence and of carrying the fight (there *is* a fight) to the enemy (there *is* an enemy). Coleridge thought 'strict accuracy of expression' both a moral responsibility and a powerful resource in times of 'vicious phraseology' and 'corrupt eloquence'. It would help, he believed, 'in the preclusion of fanaticism, which masters the feelings more especially by indistinct watchwords' (*BL*, 228, 229, 230). The opposite view is Tony Blair's. Asked on the *Today* programme whether he now regretted using the phrase 'the war on terror', he answered: 'It hardly matters what language we use.'[6]

The 'airy nothing' that pre-exists the poem cannot be given shape and a habitation in abstractions. In the process of being written it must pass from being unknown, airy, and nothing into being something substantially knowable by the senses. The young Hölderlin, while still in thrall to his mentor Schiller, wrote several poems mostly in rhyming trochees and of many stanzas addressed to such abstractions as Immortality, Freedom, Humanity, Beauty, Friendship, The Spirit of Youth, which are full of fervour and not weighted by precise realities. He soon moved on from that into a poetry which, still lifting up, realized its hopes and disappointment in the facts and material of where and when, really and imaginatively, he lived. His poetry's local habitations are Swabia, Switzerland, Ancient Greece, places in France he walked through on the verge of insanity. Many of his late poems are, like van Gogh's fields, sunflowers, irises, and almond blossom, terrifying in their immanent particularity. But that process, if not into madness, is the way it has to be: ever more immanently here and now. Poetry lives and moves in what Blake called 'minute particulars'.[7] It may of course treat abstractions; but only by realizing them concretely and particularly will it make them, in Hölderlin's phrase, 'fühlbar und gefühlt' [feelable and felt].[8] Carlos Williams's dictum 'No ideas but in things'[9] cannot be always and universally applied (no dicta on poetry should be) but is a useful warning against rapture. Every poem, like Antaeus, must keep at least one foot on the ground.

Poetry deals with the largest issues—birth, love and death, and all the good and bad things that are done or just happen in the time allowed. Poetry was and is still there in all the vast horrors we have perpetrated upon our planet and on our fellow creatures and also in the courage and solidarity of our efforts at redress. But to treat such large matters effectively, which is to say tellingly so that they are brought home as felt truths into the reader's heart, poetry must concentrate, it must be concrete, particular, local, and its characters, those suffering or rejoicing, those acting well or badly, must have faces. When newscasters issue their warning that some listeners, some viewers, may find the following interview or the following images distressing, they acknowledge in so doing the power of particularities: the Somali woman recounting her rape, the babies in the camps gazing at us through the flies, these are what it means in particular, this is the thing in person. We can bear abstractions, we can bear the statistics, we can't bear a particular woman's voice nor one infant's swarming eyes.

Since its beginnings, poetry in Britain and Ireland has been notable for its attentiveness to the real details of life on earth. Attending like that, poets became good at saying what their senses apprehended of the natural and man-made world, of their lives in it, and of the lives that its flora and fauna share with them. Chaucer identifies his pilgrims, his 'compaignye / Of sondry folk', by dress, speech, physical appearance, and demeanour, with wonderfully quick finesse. The Knight, for example: 'Of fustian he wered a gypon / Al bismotered with his habergeon'; and the Prioress's French and her table manners:

> And Frenssh she spak ful faire and fetisly,
> After the scole of Stratford atte Bowe,
> For Frenssh of Parys was to hire unknowe.
> At mete wel ytaught was she with alle;
> She leet no morsel from hir lippes falle,
> Ne wette hir fyngres in hir sauce depe;
> Wel koude she carie a morsel and wel kepe
> That no drope ne fille upon hire brest.
> In curteisie was set ful muchel hir lest.
> Hir over-lippe wyped she so clene
> That in hir coppe ther was no ferthyng sene
> Of grece, whan she dronken hadde hir draughte.
> Ful semely after hir mete she raughte.

The Miller has one of those 'distinguishing marks' that used to be required on your passport:

> Upon the cop right of his nose he hade
> A werte, and theron stood a toft of herys,
> Reed as the brustles of a sowes erys;
> His nosethirles blake were and wyde.[10]

We can't know whether Chaucer ever actually saw such a nose on such a miller. Seems likely, but we can't know for certain. But whether he did or didn't, the nose *in that particular view of it* did not exist in poetic fact, not even for Chaucer, and was thus an airy nothing, until he housed it in exactly those words. In Classical and Renaissance poetics the process of composition was understood as the clothing of a subject (*res*) in words (*verba*), a sort of incarnation. Even such a drastically physical thing as the Miller's nose is, as poetic subject, immaterial until clothed and incarnated in words. Poets give to airy nothings, which might be a warty nose or The Spirit of Freedom,[11] a local habitation by wording them. It happens that along the main line of the British poetic tradition the subjects have been more of the former kind than the latter. In choosing its subjects and in treating them the English tradition has for the most

part avoided abstractions. It is not, at its most characteristic, a cereb-
ral poetry either; it is sensuous, intelligently sensuous (that mixture
in, for example, Donne).[12]

There have been modes in English poetry that moved away from
this ground, of course, but never for so long or so damagingly as,
thanks to the Academy, in the poetry of France. The clearest and
strongest line in British and Irish poetry is earthly. Even its priestly
writers—Herbert, Hopkins, R. S. Thomas—are, as poets, what the
Germans call 'diesseitig', they are on this side, not 'jenseitig' (gone
beyond), they practise in the here and now. The mystics also are
notably earthly. Vaughan and Traherne, quite as much as the
painter Samuel Palmer, saw their own localities in a visionary
light. The language of the 'metaphysical' poets, whatever their sub-
jects (bed or God) is tough, wiry, 'nervous' (sinewy, vigorous, for-
cible), their famous conceits are, most typically, as exact and concrete
as they are ingenious: Donne's 'gold to ayery thinnesse beate', is still
gold, finely teased out of the solid. This natural allegiance to the
things of the earth is a powerful help in ushering the conception of
a poem into adequate shapes and forms. You will more easily find
those immaterial beginnings a local habitation if you have one your-
self, if you belong somewhere, if you love and feel loyalty towards
'the very world, which is the world / Of all of us,—the place where
in the end / We find our happiness, or not at all.'[13] English-language
poetry—massively afforced after Whitman by that of North
America—has as its birthmark and chief blessing the sensuous love
of 'the very world'.

In the *Biographia Literaria*, coming again and again at the questions
still working in him from his association with Wordsworth and the
Lyrical Ballads, Coleridge charted the line of language in English
verse that Wordsworth called 'the real language of men' and wished
all poetry to adopt. And to characterize it, he translated remarks
made by the German critic Christian Garve on the diction of the
poet, his compatriot, Christian Gellert: 'It was a strange and curious
phenomenon...to read verses in which everything was expressed
just as one would wish to talk, and yet all dignified, attractive, and
interesting; and all at the same time perfectly correct as to the meas-
ure of the syllables and the rhyme.'[14] It doesn't matter whether or
not a modern reader of Gellert would feel that to be true. Such

judgements are relative to the language poets have used in the native and foreign traditions before and since. And we can agree with Coleridge that this relative plain-speaking should by no means be poetry's only option. But a tone and a register are being described by Garve which we ourselves will recognize, as far as English verse is concerned, not just in Wordsworth but also, certainly, in writers such as Chaucer and Herbert whom Coleridge places in the lineage before him. It is the mainstream and a very great resource in English verse.

It was largely because Wordsworth had reconnected British poetry to the—by the Augustans—interrupted tradition of the '*lingua communis*' that British poets did better than their German counterparts at saying what the First World War was like. They could more easily accommodate the real details of modern warfare—the gas, the duckboards, the whizzbangs—into their verse than could the Germans whose tradition of plain-speaking in poetry was far less well established and much more fragmentary. Apollinaire could do it in French because Baudelaire, Rimbaud, and Verlaine had before him wrenched the language out of the hands of the Academy into something nearer to common parlance. Rimbaud's line 'On n'est pas sérieux, quand on a dix-sept ans' leaps back across three or four centuries, to Ronsard or Villon, for its connection with the tone of real speech. It is nonetheless an alexandrine, just as Donne's 'What I will say, I will not tell thee now' is a monosyllabic iambic pentameter: the exact tone of real speech in poetic form. In the English tradition that tone, that matching of common speech to the line of verse, is never absent for very long. I guess everyone will have their own anthology of such beauties: 'So have I heard and do in part believe it'; 'When he was here / He did incline to sadness, and ofttimes / Not knowing why'; 'I saw Eternity the other night'; 'I try not to remember these things now.'[15] The lines have an affective force akin to that of innocence. It shocks us that truth can be so plainly said.

One thing that French Classicism particularly abhorred, Shakespeare being the worst offender, was 'le mélange des genres' [the mixing of genres]—the grave-digger in *Hamlet*, the drunken porter in *Macbeth*, for example. There are no such co-existences of high tragedy and low comedy in Corneille, Racine, or Voltaire. And in

Classical and Renaissance poetics generally three styles were recognized—high, middle, and low—each by the law of decorum deemed suitable for particular poetic subjects. So you were guided in clothing your subject appropriately—in what form, at what level—by the nature of that subject itself. English poetry, epic, dramatic, and lyric, for most of its course has been very willing and able to move between tones and registers, even within the same poetic project. This versatility springs from the English language itself, so mixed in its roots and ramifications. As is well known, you can mix the tones of verse by playing the Anglo-Saxon against the Latin: 'No, this my hand will rather / The multitudinous seas incarnadine, / Making the green one red' (*Macbeth* 2.2, 60–2). Shakespeare's total vocabulary is about 25,000 words; Racine's about 4,000. That has less to do with learning and brain-power than with the relative states of the two languages and the conventions of English Elizabethan and French Classical verse. But from the centuries before and after Shakespeare the superabundant linguistic inheritance of English poetry, its infinite variety, matches the world we actually live in, a world which is, as Louis MacNeice said (in 'Snow'), 'incorrigibly plural'. To realize their experience of that world, most poets nowadays would insist on the freedom to move where they like in the total linguistic stock (no words in it however base, elevated, coarse, technical, obsolete, childish, local, being of themselves unsuitable for poetry) and to deploy whatever resources of grammar and syntax they think fit. At least, I hope they would. One unfortunate modern tendency in English-language verse is rather to reduce the range towards the lower and wholly colloquial end; which is just as detrimental to the whole poetic enterprise as limiting yourself to purity at the top end.

The figurative

Why should a *local* habitation interest anyone but the locals? The chief sense of Shakespeare's use of the word in *A Midsummer Night's Dream* (1600) is 'relating to or concerned with "place" or position in space'. The 'airy nothing' is given a spatial presence. But the *OED* notes that from some time in the fifteenth century the word could also mean 'belonging to a particular place on the earth's surface; relating to or existing in a particular region or district'; and by

1615 'local' is recorded as having in some usages a restrictive force, that is: 'limited or peculiar to a particular place'. Poets need a sure sense of how generally telling their particularities are or can be made to be.

In the English-language tradition much poetry in many forms and in many voices has been so attached to particular localities that we cannot think of certain poets without their local habitations also at once coming to mind: Crabbe's Suffolk, for example, Clare's Fens, Wordsworth's Lakes, Emily Brontë's Pennines, Hardy's Cornwall and Dorset, Frost's New England. Norman Nicholson, of Millom in Cumberland, published a collection called *A Local Habitation*, and quoted Theseus for his epigraph. Place is a vital constituent of much of the poetry even of poets who, like Lawrence, moved restlessly across the world. He called Nottinghamshire, its coalmines among the fields, the country of his heart; but wrote of the life—his own and that of all manner of birds, beasts, and flowers—in exactly observed localities from Zennor to the shore of the Southern Ocean. Place is a ground for poetry; poems need an earth to root in. So many love poems are also poems of place.

Chaucer's Tabard Inn in Southwark was not the starting point of this locally rooted poetry—Maldon might be?—but the Prologue, with its gathering in a named and familiar place of vividly realized socially various characters, does consolidate a tradition which is perhaps the heartline of English-language poetry.

Teaching on poetry courses, I have read very many poems that can be characterized as personal and anecdotal. Typically, the writer recalls a particular occasion—it might be a walk by a lake, a concert in a cathedral, a sudden falling in love on public transport—the real factual details of which seem so compelling, so wholly to constitute the value of the occasion, that the writer feels entitled or even bound to reproduce them in the poem. I see that this assemblage of real details does not make a poem, and saying so, however gently, I have often had the hurt, indignant, or bewildered writer tell me, 'But that really is what happened!'

For my own benefit, and to try to explain myself, I set down the following at least discussable axiom: In composing a poem the poet must convert the personal, anecdotal, and accidental into the figurative. By 'figurative' I mean what I think Keats means when he suddenly remarks in his long letter to his brother and sister-in-law (18 February 1819): 'they are very shallow people who take every thing literal A Man's life of any worth is a continual allegory—and very few eyes can see the Mystery of his life—a life like the scriptures, figurative'.[16]

Bad biographies are only an assembling of (usually far too many) facts. The good ones discern and present the 'allegory' of the subject's life, its shape, its characteristic patterns, its clarified significance. Nietzsche, violently objecting to the vast positivistic biographies being produced in his day, asserted that one ought to be able to present a person's life in three anecdotes.[17] The anecdotes would of course have to be very telling, they would be emblems, luminous images you might turn this way and that and see ever more of the man or woman whose life you were contemplating. If the anecdotal materials in my students' poems were anecdotes such as Nietzsche had in mind, they would work poetically; indeed, each might be a poem in itself. Blake's 'minute particulars' would go into their making; but, hitting on what was typical of the person, they would carry a charge of the more generally typical—how people beyond and other than the one biographical subject suffer or shape their lives. One such story, chillingly figurative, concerns Nietzsche himself, champion of the *Übermensch*, and a cab horse being whipped by its driver on a street in Turin, 3 January 1889. Nietzsche intervened—he pushed through the crowd, embraced the horse's neck, and clung there sobbing. That event was the onset of his madness. He lived another ten years, speechless. And if I had to characterize Sir Maurice Bowra in three anecdotes, one of them would be this. Beginning my D.Phil. on Hölderlin, I was laboriously teaching myself Greek. Bowra offered me tutorials on Pindar. At the end of the last he took a Liddell and Scott off his shelf and with both hands—it is a heavy lexicon—he gave it to me, saying: 'Bought this for a friend. Friend died. You have it.' He knew the book would help, I was the beneficiary of his dead friend. It is an event I dwell on as I do on many poems, with gratitude for its clarity.

In the writing of a poem the process towards the figurative is one of clarification, of sorting out what counts and what does not count. But that clarification can only take place as part of the realization (discussed above) of what the poem is truly about. You clarify in the light of realization.

'Like the scriptures, figurative': in the Old and New Testaments there are indeed many images, scenes, and anecdotes which work in that way: King David who 'gat no heat' until they warmed him with Abishag; Christ and Mary Magdalene; Christ and Lazarus. Blake, quite rightly, read the Bible not as the threats and commandments of the bully Nobodaddy but much as he did any other great poems, fictions, and myths. Mary washing Christ's feet, or meeting him in the garden and told not to touch him, are no more events demanding our literal belief than are Priam's kissing the hands of Achilles that have killed his son, or the reunion of Hermione and Perdita. They are potent images, to which we assent. They are figurative, they enter into us, they work in the earth of us, troubling and prompting.

Most people (not just 'very few') reflecting on their own lives should be able to discern what is exemplary and paradigmatic in them: your peculiar course of life, the accidents and the shapings of it; but also, in the wider circle you are at the centre of, you see what is socially typical. Anyone born in England in 1944, for example, and still alive, has seen the rise and demise of an idea of the state— free education, free healthcare, social mobility, the lessening of the gap between rich and poor. You see the loss not just of a structure but also of an ethos, an idea of the *res publica*, which you had thought, once established, would be valued for ever and at all costs protected, as something no just society could go on without. You see in that one aspect of the allegory of your life.

Poets do well to let the socially figurative sense of their lives arise of itself out of the details that become most present to them when they write. This is Tony Harrison's way in the fifty (Meredithian) sonnets from *The School of Eloquence* that make up the volume *Continuous* (1981). His early life and his memories of it are very typical of the working-class boy who is the first in the family to go to grammar school. His experience is commonplace, like most of the best material of poetry. But he writes about it as though it were unique to him. And he is right in that conviction. His life is indeed unique to him; but at the same time it is paradigmatic, and by writing so well, with such painfully close attention, he lets readers see the allegory of

his life; and those who have lived at all similarly will feel he is writ-
ing of and for them and those to whom this life is a foreign country
will be admitted into it and their own lives will be enlarged.

Brecht, known chiefly (after the later 1920s) as a politically
engaged writer, led an 'exemplary' life[18] in the sense that the course
and shape of it were throughout profoundly affected by events in his
nation and in the world. For all his often vehemently asserted indi-
viduality, he led a life which was in large measure typical; and as a
writer he more and more consciously drew attention to that typical-
ness. Born 1898, just escaping active service in the First World War,
he was a close witness of much of its aftermath: the November
Revolution, Kapp Putsch, Hitler Putsch, hyper-inflation, the increas-
ingly violent polarization of politics during the later years of the
Weimar Republic, the collapse of the markets in 1929. And in 1933,
immediately after the Reichstag Fire, he went into exile. Post-war
then, he was uneasily at home in the new German Democratic
Republic. During the uprising of June 1953 there was fighting on
the Chausseestrasse, almost under his window. Some in the West
(unfairly, I think) thought him the exemplar of compromise. He died
in 1956, a couple of months before the failed revolution in Hungary.
Millions of people lived through or died in the events of that half
century. Every one of those lives has its figurative sense. Brecht had
eyes to see that sense and in his writings he made it clear. He
appears, very often in the third person, as an emblematic figure: the
playwright, the teacher, the exile; or as a named personage: Bidi,
poor B.B., Me Ti, Herr Keuner.

Clare lost the country of his childhood behind Enclosure, and in
that country was his childhood sweetheart, Mary Joyce. Small won-
der he viewed his life poetically as Paradise Lost. Further alienated
then by the fame the poems brought him, he was transported from
home to Matthew Allen's asylum at High Beach in Epping Forest,
and after that to Northampton General Lunatic Asylum, Hell being
his word for both those places. Escaping from the first, walking back
to Northborough, he wrote: 'Returned home out of Essex & found
no Mary.' She was dead by then, which he refused to believe. To
him she was 'abscent every where'. And he was 'homeless at home'.[19]
Clare's account of that escape and homecoming, 'Reccolections &c
of Journey from Essex', is a mythic document.

Hölderlin saw himself figuratively as 'the wanderer', forbidden to settle either at home or abroad; and after his last and longest journey, returning from Bordeaux in 1802 and finding that Susette Gontard had died, he commented, 'and as is said of heroes, I can surely say of myself, that Apollo has smitten me' (VI, 432). Apollo, god of poetry, flayed the satyr Marsyas alive for daring to compete with him. He was also the sun-god: Hölderlin came through France in the summer heat, much of the way on foot, and arriving among his friends and family, they thought him raving mad.

Gérard de Nerval noted, 'J'arrange volontiers ma vie comme un roman' [I do like to order my life as though it were a novel]. The essential plot of the novel was that of an ordeal and an initiation into mysteries, a quest, a descent into hell. Like Lucius (in *The Golden Ass*), he was passing through torments into the priesthood of Isis. He wrote, 'Je me jugeais un héros vivant sous le regard des dieux' [I thought myself a hero living under the eyes of the gods].[20] Everything in such a life *matters*. Sleepless, walking the streets of Paris, all his encounters were symbolic and mythic.

Clare, Hölderlin, and Nerval lived tragic myths, exciting pity and terror. They discerned and acted in accordance with the allegory of their lives long before their biographers studied them. Scenes from their or from other poets' lives—Keats at Lulworth, Akhmatova in the prison queues in Leningrad, for example—may enter our own with iconic and figurative force. Anyone in a lifetime might assemble a personal mythology of that kind and set the night sky with such chosen constellations.

We need the icons clarified out of other people's lives, for comfort, encouragement, inspiration, warning; and of course it is not necessary that they be famous and important people. We invent our mythologies out of all walks of life, from home and abroad, from among the living and the dead. This quintessentially poetic need and faculty inhabits all human beings. We invent and pay heed to stories; scenes from them lodge in us lifelong. Inventing a life-myth is something everyone does—more or less beneficially or harmfully.

The root sense of 'to invent' is 'to find'. 'The Invention of the True Cross' means the discovery, the finding of it. *Inventio* in rhetoric and the older poetics was the finding of illustrative instances, the *topoi*, the commonplaces. You did not make them up, they were there to be found, and you knew, or could learn, where to look. That meaning of 'invention' has lapsed from current English in favour of 'ingenuity, originality, the making (or making up) of something entirely new'. The Romantic Imagination, in Coleridge's definition, is inventive in that sense. He leaves to Fancy the mere combining and aggregating of the 'fixities and definites' that already exist (*BL*, 145–6). In poetic practice, however, there may not be much distinction between the root and the current usage of 'to invent'. Many poets understand the composition of the poem as a process by which an already existent thing is uncovered, brought to light. Robert Graves, for example: 'A true poem is best regarded as already existing before it has been composed: with composition as the act of deducing its entirety from a single key phrase that swims into the poet's mind.'[21]

Form itself is an invention, in both the older and in the usual modern sense. And form, taken out of an existent stock (sonnet, villanelle, ghazal, etc.) or made up by the poet for the particular task in hand, is a necessary agent in the process of converting the accidental, personal, and anecdotal into the figurative. Metre, lineation, stanzas, or whatever other devices you employ are the signs and the means of an attempt to do more than recount biographical facts. Such facts will remain just that—biographical—in verse that has no shape. The effort of shaping alerts the poet to what the poem itself actually requires. Formal shaping helps you into the figurative. You begin to see that the poem, however personal the stuff of it may be, is not itself a personal thing. You can't get at the truth of the poem, at the truth of the project in hand, and you will never extend its reach, by adhering with slavish fidelity to the accidentals out of which it sprang.

So we have this paradox: without 'minute particulars' the figurative as I mean it here cannot be achieved. Only such details will fasten us to the subject. Once fastened, we discern and are affected by the typical, figurative, general—in specific form.[22]

I wrote a poem about two houses, one in Scilly, the other in the Drôme, which, I saw afterwards, works in this dynamism of the particular and the general and optimistically expects readers to enter its stanzas, as into rooms of their own.

The House

You won't forget the house
Will you? I never will.
The south wind rattled the sash
And rain came in on the sill

And the wind denuded the moon
White and the white of the tide
Wheeling into the wind
Lifted, showed and frayed

And the sun came out of the sea
And all that way across
Easily found the house,
The bed, the looking-glass.

Remember the house so well
That somebody else elsewhere
Will say, 'We had a house
The same as where you were

But a hundred miles from the sea
And it was the north that blew
And the sky was as sheer as steel
And everything flared and flew

Stubble went down the wind
The oaks were filled with a voice
And the stars in the Milky Way
Screamed like a slide of ice

And the sun that found our bed
Rose over oaks and a hill
But the house was surely the same
Except for the sash and the sill

And there was a looking-glass
And though they were mine and hers
The faces shown by the sun
Might have been hers and yours

You remember it all so well
That except for the south and the sea
That was surely the house
Except for her and me.'

Here is a version of Sappho's 'Fragment 31', written originally in
the Greek of Lesbos in the seventh century BC:

> Gods are not happier than I think he
> Must be who sits before you face to face
> Listening closely to your every word
> Beloved girl I
>
> See how he loves to hear your laughter, my
> Beloved laughing girl, it hurts my heart
> When I see you I cannot speak, nothing
> Comes to me to say
>
> My tongue is tied and at the sight of you
> I have the sensation of fine fire
> My eyes are blinded and there is the din of
> Deafness in my ears
>
> The sweat streams down me cold, I am shaken
> Through and through and look lanker than the grass
> In summer. I think I cannot bear much more,
> My life will fail me.

Jealous love then doubtless felt much as it does now. We feel kith
and kin with her because of the details by which—in strict form
(Sapphics)—she realizes a human condition. They are what hits
home across more than two and a half millennia. The jealous
woman becomes the *Gestus* of jealousy. She is exemplary—
'musterhaft', as Goethe said of himself and Marianne von Willemer
when he and she together made poetry of their love: 'musterhaft in
Freud und Qual' [exemplary in joy and pain].[23]

Blake says of Chaucer's pilgrims: 'Some of the names or titles are
altered by time, but the characters themselves for ever remain unaltered,
and consequently they are the physiognomies or lineaments of universal
human life, beyond which Nature never steps. Names alter, things never
alter.' But our feeling that these people are types—that we might still
meet such a person as the Miller—is due to our having had so keen a
sense of him in his particularity. And Blake himself in that description of
his own fresco of the pilgrims repeatedly draws attention to the peculiari-
ties by which Chaucer gives his pilgrims a lasting life.[24]

Out of the interplay, or it may be the fighting, of the personal and
the exemplary comes a unique self-identity. Becoming the one you

are entails both. Which is why in a very real sense poetry offers, not an after-life, but a living connection down the human chain.

For somebody else, elsewhere

It is by achieving the figurative that a poem, rooted in particular circumstances, addressing them, extends also beyond them and so also beyond the life and personality of the poet. The poem is of his or her making, derives from and pertains to her or his real life, but also exceeds that life and touches on the lives of others. Since Romanticism we know, in many cases, a great deal about the real lives of the men and women who wrote the poems we still read today. In *Goethes Leben von Tag zu Tag* (Zürich, 1982–96) [Goethe's life from day to day], in its eight volumes of seven or eight hundred pages each, you can find out where he went, who he met, what he did, what he wrote, most days and at many particular hours of his long life. Such knowledge *may* be helpful in reading some poems. But clearly we don't *need* it or we could not be affected by the poems of poets—like Sappho—about whose lives we know very little or nothing at all. The poem in that sense is impersonal; and some poets—Eliot, for example—have insisted on impersonality as a chief characteristic and virtue of poetry. Poetry may derive very intimately indeed from the writer's own real experience and yet, in its practice, in its effects, be an escape from, not the expression of, personality.

Poetry is for somebody else, however personal and particular the factors in its making might be. Robert Graves called it 'the profession of private truth'. The word 'private' comes from the Latin *privare*, which means to deprive. When a thing is made private, other people are deprived of it. Enclosure did that. Our privatizations work similarly: the many are deprived of something by the few and may be allowed some use of it on terms advantageous to those few. I only quoted half of Graves's definition. In full it reads: 'Poetry is the profession of private truth, supported by craftsmanship in the use of words.'[25] By that craftsmanship, using words which are in common ownership, the personal can be converted into the figurative in a poem. Becoming a poem, the private truth is made a public good.

Against 'Art for Art's Sake', Lawrence called his own writing 'art for my sake';[26] Walt Whitman, whom he admired, wrote the 'Song of Myself'. And many other writers might say the same: this is for my sake, this poem is for my own good, I have to write it. Yes, of course. But in so far as poems, stories, novels, plays 'for my sake', become art, to that degree, they are also, and as time passes ever more so, for somebody else. Many poems are addressed to uniquely particular people. They were handed over, posted, emailed, read aloud, whispered on the pillow to a certain woman or man. Nevertheless the poem you write ceases to be personally yours by virtue of its being a poem at all, by its entry into a language which you may be more or less good at handling, which you may—indeed must—use in ways quite peculiar to you, but which does not belong to you: you participate in it, as do your readers. And as soon as you publish or broadcast or in any other way circulate the poem you have made, very obviously then it is not your property. Your name may adhere to it and you may perhaps be legally able to defend your copyright in it; but over how it is read, which is what the poem is for—to be read or listened to—over that you have no control whatsoever. This struck me as a wonderfully extending and liberating thought some years ago, and not with reference to poetry but to the music and song in the film *The Buena Vista Social Club*: the band convening again, old men with skill and passion singing love songs. My thought was: it is for somebody else, they are enjoying themselves, they are good at what they do, they are body and soul present in it, they are old, they will be dead soon, it is for somebody else. Hölderlin, in the ruins of his personal life, compressed this consolation into three short lines of a long and unfinished poem addressed to the Madonna. Almost incidentally, as it seems (the context is very fragmented), he turns from her to poetry itself and parts its life from his: 'ich zwar / Ich sterbe, doch du / Gehest andere Bahn...' [True, I / Will die, but you / Go another way...]. There it is, broken over the line-ends, stark and courageous. No one would want the suffering for such a consolation. And you don't have to think you will be among the English poets after your death to love and be grateful for those broken lines. 'Ich zwar, / Ich sterbe, doch du...' The poem exceeds the poet, exceeds the present reader too, goes on its own way, also and always for somebody else, some further human being, elsewhere.

Metaphorically speaking, the poem being written or read allows or even requires its writer or reader *to become someone else*. Keats in his letters often reverts to the question of identity: the making of it and the loss of it into the identities of others. He detected in himself, and advanced as necessary in a poet, a capacity for self-annihilation. Meeting the attractive Jane Cox ('not a Cleopatra; but...at least a Charmian') he said of the effect that her type ('such a woman') had on him, 'I am at such times too much occupied in admiring to be awkward or on a tremble. I forget myself entirely because I live in her' (162). Which recalls what he had written to his friend Bailey the year before: 'if a Sparrow come before my Window I take part in its existince and pick about the Gravel' (38). Further:

> When I am in a room with People if I ever am free from speculating on creations of my own brain, then not myself goes home to myself: but the identity of every one in the room begins so to press upon me that, I am in a very little time annihilated – not only among Men; it would be the same in a Nursery of children...(158)

Already in December 1817 he had expounded his now-famous idea of '*Negative Capability*, that is when man is capable of being in uncertainties, Mysteries, doubts, without any irritable reaching after fact & reason' (43). Later he cast his friend Dilke as the type of man 'who cannot feel he has a personal identity unless he has made up his Mind about every thing'. Better, thought Keats, is 'to make up one's mind about nothing—to let the mind be a thoroughfare for all thoughts. Not a select party' (326). The poetical character, which 'is not itself—it has no self—it is every thing and nothing—It has no character...' (157), such a mind or character, 'remaining content with half knowledge' (43), is one capable of withholding judgement, of entertaining possibilities, of allowing itself in disinterested empathy to participate in other lives. This is the faculty that enables Shakespeare to enter without prejudice (but with delight) into the lives of characters as morally far apart as Imogen and Iago. Of itself, such self-abnegating involvement is quite amoral; which is why Keats comments: 'What shocks the virtuous philosopher, delights

the camelion Poet' (157). Reading poetry, you are moved to partici-
pate imaginatively, and in that degree assent to, ways of being
human which you cannot and might not like to experience in fact.
Every human self is circumscribed by the facts of its particular exist-
ence; and further by its own ideas and creeds. Poetry extends the
biographical self first imaginatively and then, perhaps, really, beyond
its determined frontiers. A Poet, says Keats, 'has no Identity' (157).
Most poets, in fact, Keats included, have very strong self-identities,
and live accordingly. But on that basis, at heart knowing what they
and their poetry need, they go out, as it were self-annihilatingly, into
other people's lives, essaying other ways of being human.

Notes

1. Goethe, *Dichtung und Wahrheit*, Book 16.
2. Quotations from Shakespeare throughout are from the Arden edition of his
   works.
3. Bertolt Brecht, *Der gute Mensch*, Scene I.
4. Robert Graves, *Poetic Craft and Principle* (London: Cassell, 1967), 8.
5. Rainer Maria Rilke, *Werke*, 6 vols. (Frankfurt: Insel Verlag, 1982), V, 263.
6. See Orwell's 'Politics and the English Language', written in 1946, in George
   Orwell, *Collected Essays* (London: Secker & Warburg, 1961), esp. 353, 362–5.
7. Especially in *Jerusalem*: 'Labour well the Minute Particulars…'; 'For Art & Sci-
   ence cannot exist but in minutely organized Particulars'; '& every Minute Par-
   ticular is Holy', in *Complete Writings*, ed. Geoffrey Keynes (Oxford: Oxford
   University Press, 1979), 687 and 708.
8. Friedrich Hölderlin, *Sämtliche Werke*, ed. Friedrich Beissner and Adolf Beck, 8 vols.
   (Stuttgart: Kohlhammer, 1943–85), IV, 243. All further references to Hölderlin
   are to this edition and I include them in my text.
9. William Carlos Williams, in his poem 'A Sort of Song'.
10. Chaucer, 'General Prologue', ll. 24–5; 75–6; 124–36; 554–7.
11. See Chapter 5, under 'Humane letters in war and peace', on Paul Éluard's poem
    'Liberté'.
12. See Chapter 4 at n. 5, on 'reflective emotion' or 'a single tone'.
13. Wordsworth, 'French Revolution', in *The Poetical Works of Wordsworth* (Oxford:
    Oxford University Press, 1959), 165–6.
14. Coleridge, *BL*, 194; and see also Edward Thomas's review of Robert Frost's *North
    of Boston*: '[He] has, in fact, gone back, as Whitman and as Wordsworth went
    back, through the paraphernalia of poetry into poetry again. With a confidence
    like genius, he has trusted his conviction that a man will not easily write better
    than he speaks when some matter has touched him deeply'—in Matthew Hollis,
    Now All Roads Lead to France (London: Faber and Faber, 2011), 148.

15. Arthur Rimbaud, 'Roman'; Donne, 'The Apparition'; Shakespeare, *Hamlet*, 1.1, 170; *Cymbeline*, 1.7, 61–3; Henry Vaughan, 'The World'; Owen, 'The Sentry'.

16. *The Letters of John Keats*, ed. Robert Gittings (Oxford: Oxford University Press, 1970), 218. Keats's letters are referred to throughout in this edition, hereafter simply by page number in brackets after the quotation in my text.

17. Nietzsche, the (later) Foreword to 'Die Philosophie im tragischen Zeitalter der Griechen', in *Werke*, ed. Karl Schlechta, 5 vols. (Berlin: Ullstein, 1981), III, 1059.

18. On this question of 'exemplary' lives consider the *Vitae*, the Lives of Saints, in which there is an extreme reduction and shaping of the biographical material into the typical and figurative. And on the uniqueness of individual human experience (Hardy at Boscastle) see Chapter 4, under 'Saying the human'.

19. *The Prose of John Clare*, ed. J. W. and Anne Tibble (London: Barnes and Noble, 1970), 244 and 250. For 'abscent every where' see 'Song' ('O Mary dear three springs have been...').

20. Gérard de Nerval, *Aurélia*, ed. Jean Richer (Paris: Minard, 1965), 172. And *Aurélia*, in *Oeuvres complètes* (Paris: Pléiade, 1993), III, 740.

21. Robert Graves, *Mammon and the Black Goddess* (London: Cassell, 1965), 74.

22. See Louis MacNeice's Note to his collection *Springboard* (London: Faber and Faber, 1944): 'Many of my titles...have the definite article, e.g. "The Satirist", "The Conscript". The reader must not think that I am offering him a set of Theophrastean characters. I am not generalising; "The Conscript" does not stand for all conscripts but for an imagined individual; any such individual seems to me to have an absolute quality which the definite article recognises.' The poem, in my understanding, makes the individual figurative by, and only by, fully acknowledging his or her unique individuality (the 'absolute quality').

23. In the poem 'Wiederfinden', in the collection, *Der West-östliche Divan*.

24. Blake, *Complete Writings*, 567. The whole description: 566–75.

25. Graves, *Poetic Craft and Principle*, 26.

26. D. H. Lawrence, in a letter of 24 December 1912 to Ernest Collings.

2
Translation

How much a nation translates is in part a measure of how much it feels it needs to have its native literature and culture enriched or relativized by the foreign. Nations are more or less self-confident, and the index of that confidence rises and falls in the course of their history. Much of German literature in the seventeenth century was made *by main force of translation*: by the appropriation of novels, plays, and poetry in all the genres from the more self-confident nations, Italy, Spain, France, England, and from the Classical past. France and Britain have been notably self-confident nations, sure of their physical borders within which their languages are spoken, sure of their literary traditions. In the case of Britain that confidence has for some time now done more harm than good. More than three hundred languages are spoken at home in London today; but the public and international aspect of the United Kingdom is monoglot, insular, and, often, xenophobic. We ride on the quite false assumption that the English language is our entrée everywhere. It really isn't, nor should it be. Of the total number of books published yearly in the UK only about three per cent are translations (same in the USA). In our schools and universities the teaching of modern languages has been sidelined and diminished. We are as a nation shamefully ignorant about the countries we invade or trade with. (Most Arab countries translate even less than we do, to their obvious grave detriment.)

Of the seven volumes of Rilke's collected works, one, a very substantial volume, is given over entirely to his translations; in the case of Paul Celan, translations take up two volumes out of five. For both poets translation was an integral and important part of their whole oeuvre. Neither translated to make a living; both translated poets who mattered to them, from whom they could learn, whose language being put into German could benefit their own. Much of their work as translators has been studied by scholars; poets might study it with even greater benefit. You see what in the hands of a first-rate poet a native tongue is capable of in dynamic dealings with the foreign. Also, how a poet's own mythology may be enriched by appropriating figures from abroad. Rilke translated all forty-four of Elizabeth Barrett Browning's sonnets that she had offered to the public as being 'from the Portuguese'. He fetched her across—as figure, as exemplar—into his pantheon of women in love; and in a language entirely his own, in a form (the son-net) that he practised in abundance and variety throughout his writing life, he articulated another tone of the voice of feeling.

In the winter of 1798–9, while Coleridge, first in Ratzeburg then in Göttingen, flung himself idiosyncratically into learning German, Wordsworth sealed himself off with Dorothy in great discomfort in Goslar and got on with his own compositions there—beginning *The Prelude*—much as he might have in Grasmere. It may be that the 'wordsworthian or egotistical sublime' sort of poet needs the foreign less than other sorts. And does it matter that Larkin hated 'abroad'? (I think it does.) There are today important British and Irish poet-translators, thoroughly knowledgeable in the languages from which they translate, but they are the exceptions. Other poets seek a con-nection with the foreign—in space and time—and get it through existing translations. But many don't, and perhaps do not feel the lack. Nor do all poets writing in the UK now pay very much atten-tion even to their own country's poetic tradition. Indeed, for several contemporary poets in multicultural Britain that tradition is a dubi-ous, difficult, and *very* foreign thing.

I can only say that translation—from abroad and out of the past—seems to me both necessary and deeply beneficial. Really, for myself, I could not do without it. It is part of my belief that poetry is larger, more connected, more far-reaching than the poet. I want my own dialect and my own local habitation and my few years in the twentieth century and fewer in the twenty-first to belong, how-ever insignificantly, to a wide and various republic of letters.

Understanding

Translation has to do with understanding. People who know noth-ing about translation sometimes wonder why it is said to be so difficult. Surely if you know two languages, your mother tongue and another, you know the matching words in each and may simply replace a word in *Language a* with its match in *Language b*? Or if you happen not to know the match, you will find it in a dictionary. In practice, even at the simplest level such 'horizontal' replacements will not get you very far; but I can explain better what I mean by 'understanding' if I move at once to an instance of real difficulty: Michael Hamburger's translations of Paul Celan. Hamburger, born in Berlin, his mother tongue German, emigrated with his family to Britain in 1933 at the age of nine and learned English so well that seven years later he was looking for a publisher for his translations of Hölderlin. He became thoroughly bi-lingual, and did almost all of his writing, including poetry, in English. As a translator of German, he, if anyone, surely had no lexical difficulties. His understanding in that sense (allowing for the blindspots that every translator inherits or acquires in living) was near perfect. But he translated Celan, over two decades, *only as his understanding of the poems progressed.* In 1984, 'thanks only to those flashes of recognition or comprehension that come from repeated readings of the text', he found himself able to do some thirty of Celan's later poems which, for one reason or another, had defeated him in earlier attempts. Then, proceeding successfully, he reached the short poem 'Coagula', the last word of which in German is 'Kolben', and there he was halted. He writes, 'It was the last word that told me I did not know what the whole poem was about, though I had translated it up to the last word.'[1] Clearly, he knew what his lexical possibilities were—'Kolben' means several things: rifle-butt, plunger, piston, spadix, and more besides— but he could not honestly make a choice among them, because his understanding of the context had not advanced enough. So he waited, bided his time, carried on reading, made enquiries, came back again and again. Then arriving at an understanding (which needless to say has no absolute claim, but is the understanding that he in all conscience by dint of much study made his), he settled on 'rifle-butt', finished the translation of the poem and included it in the next edition of his Celan. Hamburger at work on Celan is a good enactment of the phrase I quoted at the outset almost as the watchword of this little book and of all my writing about poetry: 'knowledge in the making'.

Translation widens and deepens understanding. Many of the texts we translate are not only foreign by country and language but most often we bring them across also out of the past, which is itself a foreign country where they do things differently. Translation works across frontiers of space and time. It makes an international Republic of Letters, goods go between its federated states across the centuries in free exchange. This is beneficent globalization, fair dealings of the living and the dead, all manner of tongues, all manner of peoples giving and receiving, for the increase of understanding. We can't live well in the here and now without close and living connection with the there and then—without abroad, without the past. In fact, we greatly reduce our chances of bare survival if we won't go abroad and into the past for understanding. And it will become clear, I hope, that the understanding I think so necessary is not at all a flattening of differences in the interest of easy access. On the contrary, it means recognizing and acknowledging what outside us is deeply and perhaps unalterably foreign so that in the light of it, and in lively dealings with it, we may better understand what we are ourselves, what is truly our own. Most of what I have to say about translation has to do with that: the making of self-identity in relation to others.

The free use of one's own

In earlier schools of poetry, translation was a requirement. Through the study of a foreign tongue you came into your own. Ronsard, for example, worked at Greek for twelve years, the better to handle his native French. Chaucer, Wyatt, and Surrey came into the English of their poetry through close dealings with French and Italian. Hölderlin fashioned his German through Greek, through a word-by-word, indeed syllable-by-syllable, literal version of 2000 lines of Pindar's Victory Odes. For, as he said, 'das eigene muß so gut gelernt seyn, wie das Fremde' [we have to learn what is our own as well as what is foreign]. The goal, he said, was 'der freie Gebrauch des Eigenen' [the free use of one's own] (VI, 426). Poets had to learn their trade. Like journeymen, they were required—literally or figuratively—to travel and to serve abroad.

This was a national as well as an individual onus. In the Renaissance, beginning in Italy, the vernacular languages had to assert themselves for a self-identity against the almost overwhelming status of Latin and Greek, for the present, against the past, for a present vitally involving that past. They had to discover who and what they were, what they could do, what native resources they had at their disposal. Further, there were feelings of inferiority or superiority among the moderns themselves, in their relations with one another, according to how far they had advanced in making a literature of their own. At the start of the seventeenth century German poets were very uncertain in their own tongue. They might be strong in Latin and sometimes Greek, fluent in French or Italian, but, no longer livingly connected to their great medieval heritage, they had to learn again how to frame and scan their own lines of verse, in the modern language. In England too, forty years earlier, the native language had been felt by many to be much less capable of fine expression than French, Italian, or Latin; and Sidney's *Apologie for Poetrie* (written 1580–1, published 1595) was in part an assertion of English as a fit tongue for the art. Sidney wished to settle the question of prosody: 'Now, of versifying there are two sorts, the one Auncient, the other Moderne: the Auncient marked the quantitie of each silable, and according to that, framed his verse: the Moderne, observing onely number (with some regarde of the accent)...' That is, modern verse does not scan by length of syllable as Latin and Greek do, but either (French, Italian) by number of syllables or (English, German) by those syllables being brought into a pattern of stressed and unstressed. So Sidney declared for English verse: 'though wee doe not observe quantity, yet wee observe the accent very precisely'.[2] (Even as he made that pronouncement, some among his contemporaries, notably Gabriel Harvey, were still trying to write English verse observing quantity.)

The particular matter of scansion is only one among many in a language's coming to understand and to develop itself. Every national literature must continuously engage in that process, or die. And of course every national literature is always being made by its hundreds of individual writers who are all on the move to find their own voices, fashion their own languages, in productive dealings with predecessors and contemporaries at home and abroad.

Sir Thomas Wyatt (1503–42) and his friend Henry Howard, Earl of Surrey (1517–47) both translated Petrarch (1304–74). It would

exceed my present context, but their separate renderings of his son-
net 'Amor, che nel penser mio vive e regna' (Wyatt's 'The longe
love that in my thought doeth harbar...', Surrey's 'Love that liveth
and reigneth in my thought...') are well worth studying. Particu-
larly in their accenting of the iambic pentameter, and in their
handling of the sonnet's form, they demonstrate how translation
can help a poet into his own voice and, doing so, can further the
making of a national literature. They translated other sonnets by
Petrarch and wrote sonnets of their own. Wyatt shifted from the
Petrarchan scheme (two quatrains, two tercets, rhyming abba,
abba, cde, cde) into three quatrains, most often rhyming abba,
abba, cddc, with a final couplet; Surrey to the same 3 × 4 + 2 but
rhyming abab, cdcd, efef, gg, so arriving at the form of the 'Eng-
lish' sonnet, which Shakespeare would exploit to perfection. Thus
Wyatt and his young friend Surrey, two hundred years after its
florescence in Italian, between them translated the sonnet into Eng-
lish poetry—and there it stays, still expressing a modern sensibility,
treating modern matters, still inventively shifting, which is to say
still alive and necessary.[3]

Chaucer was the first to import Dante's *terza rima* into English,
but briefly and rather inconsequentially, in Parts II and III of his 'A
Complaint to his Lady'. Wyatt took it up a century and a half later,
in three satires of about a hundred lines each. And Milton in his
translations of eighteen of the Psalms, trying several versifications,
used *terza rima* for the Second. But there was no substantial deploy-
ment of the form till the Romantics. When Byron, at the suggestion
of his lover Teresa Countess Guiccioli, wrote 'The Prophecy of
Dante' in *terza rima* in June 1819, he wondered had anyone—apart
from William Hayley (three cantos of *Inferno* in 1782)—tried the
metre in English before him. Four months later came Shelley's
'West Wind'. Interestingly, this verse form can't be said to have
been much encouraged in English by translators of Dante himself,
since they, apart from Hayley, had shied away from *terza rima* and
had gone, mostly, for blank verse instead, Henry Francis Cary being
especially effective. Keats took the three 32mo volumes of Cary's
Dante (published 1814) with him on his trek through the Lakes and
Scotland in 1818. Canto V of *Inferno*—the love of Paolo and Fran-
cesca—haunted him.

Cary chose blank verse, the form seemed to him a form capable of sustainably conveying serious and various material, because by then it had long been tried and tested for such purposes. But blank verse was itself an invention to meet a translator's need; a translator had faced the problem set by a large and canonical foreign text in a decidedly un-English verse form and had wondered what answering form he should employ. The text: Books II and IV of Virgil's *Aeneid*; the form: Latin hexameters (which scan by quantity); the translator: Surrey. And the form he came up with for Virgil's lines was accentual unrhyming iambic pentameters—blank verse. Chaucer (out of French) had introduced five-feet iambic rhyming couplets, but Surrey, dispensing with rhyme, brought into English (and centuries later into American) poetry an extraordinarily vigorous, variable, and, for our language, *natural* measure. Here is his version of *Aeneid* II, lines 790–800:

> This having said, she left me all in tears
> And minding much to speak; but she was gone,
> And subtly fled into the weightless air.
> Thrice raught I with mine arms to accoll her neck:
> Thrice did my hands vain hold the image escape,
> Like nimble winds, and like the flying dream.
> So, night spent out, return I to my feres;
> And there wondering I find together swarmed
> A new number of mates, mothers, and men,
> A rout exiled, a wretched multitude,
> From each-where flock together, prest to pass
> With heart and goods to whatsoever land
> By sliding seas me listed them to lead.

Half a century after Surrey, George Chapman, translating Homer's Greek hexameters, first, for the *Iliad*, used colossal 'fourteeners', seven-foot iambic lines rhyming in couplets; then, for the *Odyssey*, again rhyming iambic couplets, but two feet shorter. Keats, as is well known, was deeply affected when his friend Cowden Clarke read out samples of both to him 'loud and bold' in October 1816, from the rare folio published in the year of Shakespeare's death.

Though the rhyming pentameters were taken up, much more smoothly, by Pope for *his* Homer, the fourteeners were never naturalized. It was blank verse that thrived, donated to English poetry through translation by Henry Howard, Earl of Surrey, beheaded at the age of twenty-nine.

Sonnet, terza rima, blank verse are three (among many) imports from abroad: three resources brought into English by translation. The translators were poets, not primarily interested in English Literature but in meeting specific poetic needs and in developing their own language. German poets in the seventeenth century imported the alexandrine from France via the Netherlands; and, more productively, in the latter part of the eighteenth, several verse forms and strophic forms out of Greek via Latin. All cultures have imported, more or less abundantly and more or less deliberately, at different stages of their growth; and always the receiving language adapts the import to the nature and the needs of its own self, moving from syllabic or quantitative scansion to accentual, for example, and so making something that is at once the same and very different. German alexandrines, heavily accented and with an emphatic caesura, suited the Baroque tendency to view the world in binary opposites (body/soul, earth/heaven, transience/eternity, etc.). They have none of the sinuous fluency of Racine's lines; Racine's alexandrines *read* very differently. Goethe wrote his *Roman Elegies* in elegiac couplets, a form 'translated' from the Latin elegists Propertius and Tibullus. He commented that had he chosen the *Don Juan* stanza instead, the eroticism of his verses would have been indecent. (Many of his readers thought it indecent anyway.) Form is *never* an extra in poetry and *never* is it separable from the poem's material subject. Choosing the Classical distich (hexameter + pentameter), Goethe weighed his poems' effect against what he supposed it would have been had he chosen another foreign form, Byron's English version of the Italian *ottava rima*. Goethe, and even more so Hölderlin (his alcaic and asclepiad odes, 'Pindaric' hymns, hexameters, elegiac distiches), came into the free use of their own by appropriating foreign ways of shaping speech into verse.

Poetic resources never quite die. They lapse, they cease to be serviceable, perhaps for hundreds of years they lie out of sight and out of mind. But there may again come a need for them, a poet may remember or accidentally light on them, they may be revived and not as archaisms but as newly enlivening forms. Basil Bunting, a modernist, expressed a regional (Northern) allegiance *and* dealt with the wider modern world by recovering Anglo-Saxon alliterative verse for *Briggflatts*. His own poem is a translation—a carrying over into the present—of resources still harboured in the native language. The past of that language is lengthening, its foreignness deepening. From Anglo-Saxon, through Middle English, as far as Shakespeare our poetry's past is becoming a more and more foreign country. That is why translations done by poets of texts now remote in their own tongue—*Beowulf*, *Gawain*, *Pearl*—are so valuable. Such poet-translators keep us in living touch, they may lead us back to the predecessors they have brought forward. And for themselves and their fellow-poets they offer reminders of how English verses have been made (in those three texts in three distinct ways), and perhaps might be again. I repeat: these are not archaisms, this is not an antiquarian pastime. We need the past. Losing it, we shall do no better than any other uprooted living thing.

By translating, a poet may learn a new verse form—as Shelley did terza rima, employing it then in his 'Triumph of Life'; or grasp and re-embody for his own sense, for his own existential needs, a powerful image—as he did Ugolino's Tower for his 'Tower of Famine'. More urgently still, as by elective affinity, he was drawn to Goethe's *Faust*, to his own idea of the ethos and the hero of it; and in Pisa, during the last year of his life, he tried by translation to get closer and deeper in. He re-read the text with Claire Clairmont, there to see Byron and her daughter but also passionately involved with Shelley. She had herself begun 'Germanizing' the year before and her understanding of the language was better than his. She seems to have tutored him in it, and they read Schiller and then Goethe together. She copied lines from *Faust* into her journal, among them these (1856–9), perhaps because they seemed to characterize Shelley: 'Fate's gift to him's a spirit always driving / On and on, allowed free rein, / And in its headlong striving / It overleaps the joys of earthly living…' In the notebook containing the drafts of Shelley's *Faust* there are more than a dozen sketches of sailing boats, two or three on the pages immediately after 'Walpurgis Night', the last scene he did. In June 1822 Shelley sent John Gisborne this poignant coda to his whole involvement with Goethe's text. He writes of their boating off Lerici: 'We drive along this delightful bay in the evening wind, under the summer moon, until earth appears another world. Jane brings her guitar, and if the past and the future could be obliterated, the present would content me so well that I could say with Faust to the passing moment, "Remain, thou, thou art so beautiful".[4] Three weeks later he was drowned.

The foreign may serve a larger political and national purpose too. Locating yourself abroad the better to speak of home is a well-tried satirical strategy. Then the reader must apply the foreign, which active engagement may itself sharpen the mind for the act of criticism and revolt. Brecht's 'Chinese Poems', which he derived out of Arthur Waley's translations (*170 Chinese Poems*, first published 1918), were intended for such application, in Europe in 1938. Seamus Heaney, in the midst of the Troubles (Ireland eating herself) was drawn, like Shelley but in even more dreadful fascination, to Dante's famished Ugolino: 'That sinner eased his mouth up off his meal / To answer me, and wiped it with the hair / Left growing on his victim's ravaged skull…'[5]

Not mimesis but metaphor

Some translators, Michael Hamburger was one, describe their working method as 'mimetic'. That is, in their own language they reproduce the foreign text, the way it works, as exactly as they can. In Ewald Osers's terms, they go for 'formal correspondence' rather than 'functional equivalence'. Studying Hölderlin, wishing to translate him and reading Hamburger's translations to see how *he* had gone about it, I decided against any thorough and exact 'formal correspondence' and in favour of 'functional equivalence'. Hamburger thought he could best render Hölderlin by exactly reproducing in English the forms, mostly Greek and Latin, which he had employed in German. Like Hölderlin, he adapted the Classical scansion by quantity into one by accent. But in my view, to my ear, that transfer is more effective in Hölderlin than in his translator, because the natural accent in German is heavier than it is in English. I could not feel in Hamburger's English the metres and their rhythms that are so palpable in Hölderlin's German. So I asked myself what chiefly characterizes the movement of a Hölderlin poem? And answered: tension. And tried then for an equivalent of that function, of that effect. I wanted to engender in my English the nervousness, pace, tension, and final relief that is characteristic of much of Hölderlin's verse. I understood that such drive is engendered not (of course) by slackness but by extreme strictness of composition, and I knew I must put myself under an equivalent rigour. Translating the odes, for example, I composed my lines syllabically, using for each the same number of syllables as Hölderlin had at his disposal, but not organizing them into feet as he and his translator Hamburger did. (I had Dylan Thomas in mind, whose most rapturously lyrical poems—'Fern Hill' is a good example—are composed to syllabic patterns of his own devising: at one and the same time he nails his verse down, syllable by syllable, and engenders its lift, hurry, abundance.) But more important than that discipline of counting syllables or, for other poems, imitating (but not strictly adhering to) pentameters and hexameters, or allowing myself, in the Pindaric hymns, only the same number of lines that Hölderlin used, even more important than those disciplines, pragmatically invented for each form of verse, was for me the engendering by one English means or another (chiefly syntax) at least something of the tension and the variations in texture and pace that constitute Hölderlin's poems.

In my view it is best to think of translation, and especially the translation of poetry, not as an act of mimesis but as an act of metaphor. The foreign original has to be re-incarnated in a native metaphor. Translation and metaphor both mean—the one in its Latin roots, the other in its Greek—'a carrying over'. Hölderlin, rightly, thought the lyric poem in its entirety 'eine fortgehende Metapher' [a progressive metaphor] (IV, 266) of the feeling out of which it, the poem, came. In that sense the act of poetic composition is the making of one large metaphor (which may contain other distinct individual metaphors) of the whole complex of thoughts and feelings in which the desire to write the poem was born. Understood like that, the act of poetry is itself a translation—into the necessary metaphor. Translation and metaphor equally are acts of realization, of making palpable, incarnating. In poetic-religious thinking Christ is the metaphor of God. God translates—or estranges—Himself into the foreign substance of humanity. More mundanely, to make a metaphor of a foreign poem the translator must attempt something *very* akin to the making of a poem. The successful translation would stand in relation to the foreign poem rather as a poem you write yourself does in relation to the urgent but inarticulate nexus that prompted it. I say 'rather as'; and will now indicate one critical difference.

Service and autonomy

There is an interesting and, I think, productive, paradox at the heart of translation, particularly the translation of poetry. Translation is a service, it serves a foreign text; which is why it was thought very suitable for women in the nineteenth century (the male author, the female translator) and why even today the work is so poorly paid, and so slighted that many publishers would much prefer not to have the translator's name on the cover of the book and some refuse to, and why foreign books get broadcast on the radio in English as though they had sprung there like Athena out of Zeus's head, by parthenogenesis, no mortal translator having had anything to do with it. Translation is service. In the eighteenth century it was the lowest hack work; translators were paid off and died, mostly nameless. Hans Magnus Enzensberger dedicated his *Selected Poems*, translated by Michael Hamburger (Bloodaxe Books, 1994), 'To the noble coolies of poetry, translators in East and West, with gratitude'. In practice nowadays much literary translation is service of a noble and unselfish kind. It is done by people who love the texts they are translating, who wish their authors to be better known, who believe good will come of it. Still, it is service. The page is not bare, there is a text on it, which the translator must address, is bound by, is there to serve. In that obligation and noble endeavour lie—especially if the text is a poem—the 'contraries' out of which, one hopes, progression into a translation, a fitting metaphor, will come. The poem, any poem, has and must safeguard its autonomy; it was made by a poet enjoying autonomy. To make a good translation (a good metaphor) of the original poem, the translator must make a poem. Making that new native poem he/she bids for autonomy, all the while being, by the very nature of the undertaking, in service to the foreign. That dynamic is worth studying.

Liveliness

For his literary periodical *Thalia* Schiller asked Hölderlin to do him
a translation of Ovid's 'Phaethon'. Perhaps he thought the example
of its hero might teach the young poet moderation. Hölderlin chose
the *ottava rima* stanza for Ovid's hexameters and at first enjoyed the
work. He observed, 'Man ist nicht so in Leidenschaft, wie bei einem
eigenen Producte' [One is not so impassioned as in productions of
one's own] (VI, 169); that is, he liked what he called elsewhere 'the
gymnastics' (VI, 125) of translation, the exercise that would do your
language good. Really, not too much was at stake, he could make a
workmanlike job of it, enjoying the challenges of versification. Col-
eridge, having translated Schiller's *Wallenstein*, commented on that
same experience of the dynamics of poetic translation. He said in his
second Preface to his translation, 'Translation of poetry into poetry
is difficult, because the Translator must give a brilliancy to his lan-
guage without the warmth of original conception, from which such
brilliancy would follow of its own accord.' Which is close to Höld-
erlin's 'not so impassioned'—a good state if you view the translation
as an exercise, bad if you want to do the foreign poem justice and
make a poem in your native language of it. For if working on the
foreign poem *does* engender 'the warmth of original conception' then
the fight between service and autonomy begins. Another way of
describing that fight is 'means to an end' against 'end in itself'. In
translation even the making of poetry is a means to an end: to get
the beloved and revered original across, to serve it. In composing a
poem the making of poetry is just that.

Translators have a strategy called compensation: if you fail the
expressive power of the original in one place, strive to exceed it in
another. But really in the translation of poetry your whole endeavour
is compensatory. The original is not in your language, it is not your
poem, everywhere, every line, you are searching for ways of making
up that deficit; which is to say, of making something in your language
as lively as the original is in its; and that something is a poem. You
bring, ideally, all your resources, all your experience and knowledge
of your native speech, into play for this endeavour. And in so doing,
as I said above, you engender the contraries out of which, for success,
must come progression. The struggle is worse the better you know the

language and the poet you are translating. As you realize what he or she is doing, admiring it, the less do you want to fail it in your own language. Which may be why some very reputable poet-translators are drawn to poetry in a language they don't know or don't know well, why they do 'versions', 'imitations', why they write poems 'after' the Spanish or Greek of x or y. They want elbow-room, they don't want to serve, they want autonomy. And in fact any translator-poet, deep in the work and however scrupulously serving the foreign text, always consciously or unconsciously asks the question, 'What's in it for me?' The desire is always to come into 'the free use of one's own', to be better in your native tongue; and translation, even or perhaps especially in the conflict of its demands, is a help.

Most translations don't last long. The texts themselves live for ever but only a few translations enter the corpus of the translator's language and live there among the native works. This perhaps dispiriting fact may be explained in part by the gap in talent between translators and the writers they translate. Translating great poetry, you have a lot to make up, particularly if, as I suggested above, you are trying to make a living metaphor of it, not a copy. But you can fail better if you always bear in mind that every word counts, every choice you make in syntax, word-order, register, tone, must contribute to the whole compensatory endeavour. There is statistical evidence for what one often feels about translations: that they are less *various* than the originals. There is in them, very often, a poorer deployment of the host language's lexical and grammatical possibilities, altogether less variety of utterance. And variety may be not just the spice of life but the very mark of and means to it. Translations die fast because there is, on the whole, less adventure, less risk, less departure from the norm in them than in the originals. In the case of the translation of successful novels, with a reading public in the UK and the USA, this impoverishment may even be programmatic; it may even be a publisher's directive not to be too local, not too regionally or personally idiosyncratic. Translators anyway, unless they are watchful, may drift towards a consensus—inoffensive— language; and with the market in mind they may do so consciously, towards a mid-Atlantic speech, intelligible to both sides, unsettling neither. Worse than that, I once heard a bestselling novelist say that even as he wrote he bore in mind how well or badly his words might do in translation, and trimmed accordingly. Since there is no money in poetry and less than none in translating it neither poet nor translator will be lured that way. Still the translator should always strive to be as various as the author being translated, because in that variety, the language deploying itself out of an abundance of resources, there is some hope of liveliness.

Liveliness may be particularly hard to engender if the text in question was written long ago. Not living in 1820 and not being Shelley, you can't translate his foreign contemporaries into a version of the language of Shelley. Antiquarian pastiche never works (many have tried it). You have to translate as whoever you are wherever you are here and now. On the other hand, update radically into the language of this minute, the language of the young generation on the streets right now, and your translation will be dead before it gets published. You have to write in a language neither antiquarian nor up-to-the-minute modern; which is to say a language which is, in relation to the text, equivalently poetic. A translation will survive only if it has what the language of poetry has: an abundant liveliness. And going for that, we are back in the fight between service and autonomy I described above.

The infallible test of good writing, says Coleridge (*BL*, 229), is 'its *untranslatableness* in words of the same language without injury to the meaning'. In writing a poem, you are bound to believe that certain words in a particular order in a particular rhythm are the only adequate way of saying what you want to say. No word is replaceable by any other in the language, nor will any different order do. Few poets achieve that constantly, but the belief in its possibility is what drives them. They want the poem to have what the Germans call *Endgültigkeit*, a conclusiveness, a final validity.[6] Most translation does not have that property. All too often, far more often than in writing a poem, when you look at the text again a different way of translating it will occur to you.

Translation is close reading

I have quite often conducted poetry-translation workshops for which no knowledge of the foreign language is necessary. Here is an account of one. First the poem:

Hälfte des Lebens

Mit gelben Birnen hänget
Und voll mit wilden Rosen
Das Land in den See,
Ihr holden Schwäne,
Und trunken von Küssen
Tunkt ihr das Haupt
Ins heilignüchterne Wasser.

Weh mir, wo nehm' ich, wenn
Es Winter ist, die Blumen, und wo
Den Sonnenschein,
Und Schatten der Erde?
Die Mauern stehn
Sprachlos und kalt, im Winde
Klirren die Fahnen.

The point of the exercise, whether you know German or not, is by close reading and translation to try to understand how 'Hälfte des Lebens' works, what constitutes the poetry of it. And through the foreign language we may see also what might work in a poem in English.

First I read the poem aloud

German, like English, is an *accented* language, and in fact more heavily accented than English. You will hear where the stresses fall in a line of German verse. And you may be able to hear whether the pattern of stressed and unstressed syllables is regular or not. Also, you may pick up assonance and, if the poet uses it, rhyme.

Secondly we describe the appearance and make-up of the poem

This poem has a title.
It is composed of two stanzas, each of seven lines.
The lines vary in length (typographically, number of words, number of stresses).
Glance down the last words of each line (I'll say them aloud): there are no rhymes.

Listen (I'll read one stanza again): You can probably hear that the stress-pattern is not regular.

Look at the punctuation. The first stanza is all one sentence. The second is two: its first four lines are a question, so the last three should be the answer.

You will see that most lines go over into the next to complete their sense. Enjambement: the unit of verse (the line) and the unit of grammatical sense are mostly not allowed to coincide.

Note: You can get a long way into the whole sense of a poem by accurately observing its physical make-up. You can do this (with help) even in a language you don't speak.

Translation—word-for-word

Hälfte des Lebens
Half of the life

Mit gelben Birnen hänget
With yellow pears hangs
Und voll mit wilden Rosen
And full with wild roses
Das Land in den See,
The land into the lake
Ihr holden Schwäne,
You gracious swans
Und trunken von Küssen
And drunk of kisses
Tunkt ihr das Haupt
Dip you the head
Ins heilignüchterne Wasser.
Into the holysober water.

Weh mir, wo nehm' ich, wenn
Woe me, where take I when
Es Winter ist, die Blumen, und wo
It winter is the flowers and where
Den Sonnenschein,
The sunshine
Und Schatten der Erde?
And shadow(s) of the earth?

Die Mauern stehn
The walls stand
Sprachlos und kalt, im Winde
Speechless and cold, in the wind
Klirren die Fahnen.
Clatter the weathervanes.

Some comments on the translation

German nouns have capital letters.

German word-order: verb precedes subject if the sentence or a clause begins with something other than the subject. Thus: 'With yellow pears...hangs the land into the lake'; 'in the wind / Clatter the weathervanes'. When translating you have to judge how odd it would sound in English if you reproduced a syntax which is normal and correct in German and what good or harm such oddness would do.

Some of the syntax of the poem departs from normal German usage. It is strange. In Line 2 a normal syntax would be: 'Mit gelben Birnen und voll mit wilden Rosen hänget das Land in den See.' (Or 'voll' could go to the beginning of the sentence and apply equally to the pears and the roses.)

Line 4 (right in the middle of the stanza) is an entirely disconnected apostrophe (address to the not previously mentioned swans).

Line 5 'Und' comes, so to speak, from nowhere.

Line 6 'Tunkt' is cognate with the Northern English (originally American) word 'dunk'—to dip. If you chose 'dunk' to translate 'tunkt' you would move a quite usual word into a regional or unusual one. You have to ask: what good or harm would such a shift do?

Line 7 'heilignüchtern' is a compound adjective: heilig + nüchtern. German, like Greek, can do this far more readily than can English. The author of this poem, a great translator from Ancient Greek and a passionate admirer of Ancient Greek culture, readily used the resources of his native German to get closer to Greek.

Note that 'heilig' has in it all the connotations of English 'holy'. Consider: holy, whole, hale, heal, hail (the greeting).

Line 8, first appearance of the first person—in sorrow and anxiety.

Note: Much of the pathos of the poem is contained in the grammatical relationship of question and answer which is the chief constituent of this second stanza.

Some comments on the poem

It is a poem largely composed of images: the pears and the roses hanging into the lake; the swans dipping their heads into the water; the walls, the weathervanes. In the first stanza their composite sense is equipoise, balance, reciprocity: land and water, warmth/passion with coolness and sobriety. Also of fullness: the ripe pears, the abundant roses. And you can imagine a doubling of the image of swans as they bow into the water and are reflected. It must be late summer. So this state of abundance and equipoise will not last, it is on the point of going over into autumn and winter. The 'going over' is there already in the hanging down of pears and roses—and also, an instance of form conveying sense, in the frequent enjambement: the lines themselves are toppling over. You may hear it also in the nervousness of the rhythms. The uncertainty of the syntax—the sudden apostrophe—likewise contributes to a sense of precariousness.

In the second stanza, on the introduction of a human voice in the first person, comes the desolating image of walls and weathervanes. He asks where will he find flowers in winter and sunlight and shade (that is, the lovely reciprocating things which are there in the first stanza) and for answer gets cold speechless walls and the meaningless clatter of weathervanes.

Note: there is no fair-copy of this poem. Its first appearance, completed, is in print. But on a very crowded manuscript page, containing drafts for other poems, the swans, the roses, and flowers in winter are noted, separately. It almost seems the poem came about by the chance co-existence of certain images on one page. He saw he could make a poem of them.

Context

This poem was first published in 1805. By then its author, Friedrich Hölderlin, was in worsening mental health and the following year would be committed to a clinic. Discharged from there in the summer of 1807 with 'at most three years' to live, he was accommodated in a tower in the town walls of Tübingen and lived, well looked after by a carpenter's family, till his death in 1843 at the age of seventy-three. Two halves of a life. The poem was written in 1803. Its title, and the opposing two stanzas of equal length, prefigure quite closely the shape of his life: the two halves, the going over into alienation in an unanswering world.

Possible further exercises

Translate the poem. You might do different versions: one very close, one 'freer'.

Move further away and write a poem in English that employs some or all of the poetic means employed by Hölderlin in German: two symmetrical stanzas; much enjambement; irregular metre; images that constitute a state of being; shift from 'impersonal' into the first person; question and answer. The poem might be an image of the original—same emotional tenor—or, still employing the same strategies, one having an entirely different mood and sense.

Note: a poem's strategies are imitable, they may be observed, learned, carried over (translated) into your native tongue, for your own purposes.

Reading and listening

Reading is a form of translation. We make our own living metaphor of the poem when we convert the conventional signs in which it appears on the page into sense for ourselves. This is commonplace, but marvellous nonetheless. Reading alone, we may be moved to tears, laughter, exclamations of rage or delight by signs arranged on a white page. We need no special faculty, the experience is not reserved for the expensively educated. Any willing reader may incarnate the ever-present tense of poetry. The willing listener too. Long after Keats was dead, Cowden Clarke recalled how he reacted when listening to Chapman's Homer read out loud: 'How distinctly is that earnest stare, and protrusion of the upper lip now present to me, as we came upon some piece of rough-hewn doric elevation in the fine old poet...' This, for example, from the *Iliad*, Book XIII, Poseidon riding the waves:

> From whirlepits every way
> The whales exulted under him and knew their king: the Sea
> For joy did open, and his horse so swift and lightly flew
> The under-axeltree of brasse no drop of water drew.

Or this, from the *Odyssey*, Book V, the shipwrecked Odysseus flung ashore:

> Then forth he came, his both knees faltring, both
> His strong hands hanging downe, and all with froth
> His cheeks and nosthrils flowing, voice and breath
> Spent to all use; and downe he sunke to Death.
> The sea had soakt his heart through: all his vaines
> His toiles had rackt t'a labouring woman's paines.
> Dead wearie was he.

Keats is, we might say, the poem coming to life, as delight. Clarke reports that, listening, delighted, 'he sometimes shouted'. The line 'the sea had soakt his heart through' (for which, incidentally, there is no basis in the Greek), 'had the reward of one of his delighted stares'. Keats left Clarke's house in Clerkenwell 'at the day-spring', walked in a 'teeming wonderment' the two or three miles to his lodgings at 8 Dean Street (now obliterated under London Bridge Station), wrote his 'translation' of that night's reading—hailed a messenger, and 'On the first looking into Chapman's Homer' was there for his friend when he came down to breakfast at ten that morning.[7]

That's Keats. You don't have to be Keats. 'Teeming wonderment' is open to everyone, as is, more measuredly, the ingesting of the poem into our lives. Reading or listening attentively—nothing lax, nothing sloppy, nothing self-indulgent—we may translate the poem's very precise realities into the living of our own lives. As Auden says: 'To read is to translate, for no two persons' experiences are the same.'[8] That translation of poetry and fiction into living may be very radical indeed. It is an encounter. The writing asks, 'Where were you going? Where *are* you going now that you and I have met?'

Notes

1. Michael Hamburger, 'On Translating Celan', in *Testimonies* (Manchester: Carcanet, 1989), 279–80.

2. Sir Philip Sidney, *An Apologie for Poetrie* (Cambridge: Cambridge University Press, 1948), 60–1.

3. For a fuller discussion, see my *A Living Language* (Newcastle: Bloodaxe, 2004), 22–4 and the Introduction by Gerald Bullett to the Everyman *Silver Poets of the Sixteenth Century* (London: Dent, 1970), pp. viii–xii.

4. *The Letters of Percy Bysshe Shelley*, ed. F. L. Jones, 2 vols. (Oxford: Clarendon Press, 1964), II, 435–6.

5. Seamus Heaney, 'Ugolino', in *Field Work* (London: Faber and Faber, 1979).

6. Finally beginning to write poetry, Edward Thomas wrote to Robert Frost, who had encouraged him to try, 'I find myself engrossed and conscious of a possible perfection as I never was in prose'—in Hollis, *Now All Roads Lead to France*, 195.

7. Robert Gittings, *John Keats* (London: Heinemann, 1968), 127–30—drawing on C. Cowden Clarke, *Recollections of Writers* (London, 1878), 128–30.

8. W. H. Auden, *The Dyer's Hand* (London: Faber and Faber, 1975), 3.

3

The Good of It

What is poetry *for*? What good is it? What earthly use is it? Seferis
says, 'Poetry should be strong enough to help.'[1] We have to ask,
How can it help? What is the nature of the help poetry may deliver?
I take it for granted that we do need help. Aged fifteen, Jeanette
Winterson had her first encounter with poetry when her adoptive
mother, who would only read murder mysteries, sent her to the
library to collect *Murder in the Cathedral* which she had ordered think-
ing it was one. Winterson read it there and then, and knew imme-
diately what poetry can do. She comments:

> I had no one to help me, but the T. S. Eliot helped me.
>
> So when people say that poetry is a luxury, or an option, or for
> the educated middle classes, or that it shouldn't be read at school
> because it is irrelevant, or any of the strange and stupid things that
> are said about poetry and its place in our lives, I suspect that the
> people doing the saying have had things pretty easy. A tough life
> needs a tough language – and that is what poetry is. That is what
> literature offers – a language powerful enough to say how it is.
>
> It isn't a hiding place. It is a finding place.[2]

When I try to say what poetry does and how it works, I find that
the terms I use often carry a charge of relative value. This may be
because long before I started reflecting and writing on poetry I was
certain that it mattered, that it did something valuable for me and
for anyone else who would let it; so my language when I write or
speak about poetry cannot be neutral but is unavoidably coloured
by my premise. I don't declare an *interest* in poetry—there is no
Poetry plc, you can't buy shares in it, you can't move sideways from
elsewhere and become a highly paid non-executive director on its
board—but I do declare a conviction.

Milton, in his *Areopagitica*, speaks of Adam's Fall as a way of 'knowing good by evil'; and that structure and mode of thinking, whether we like the religion of it or not, might be widely deployed. In theology, philosophy, ethics, and poetics, the way *per negativem* will often be productive. You may arrive at a clearer understanding of what a thing *is* via a clearer understanding of what it is not. More dynamically, the reality of a matter will be not just revealed but will actually be shaped by the other and contradictory realities it lives among. Nothing is, except in relation. So the nature of poetry is revealed by the social context in which it is written and read; and a large part of its value is actually engendered by that context. We can arrive at an understanding of poetic language through a better understanding of the unpoetic. And the good poetry does is good in some measure because of the bad it must contend with.

I admit, this definition through the negative may be dangerous in living and writing. Brecht knew very well that being always *against* will stunt our humanity; and poetry produced in that stance may itself, like the tree in the yard (in 'Bad times for lyric poetry'), be stunted. He writes: 'Hatred even of baseness / Distorts the features. / Anger even at injustice / Makes us hoarse...' Schiller understood Hölderlin (and 'poets like him') as the caricature-opposite of the Frankfurt mercantile world in which, as house-tutor, he was forced to earn a living; that is, he thought him produced by reaction, by defining himself *against* the world he detested. And Hölderlin feared becoming what Schiller said he already was. He wrote, 'How can a man fighting his way through a crowd and constantly being pushed to and fro maintain his poise and grace? Or keep a just measure in his feelings when the world assaults him with its fists?'[3] That state of constant oppositional reaction is an unfreedom, very bad for poets and their poetry. Still, and alas, there may be circumstances, real forces in the society and politics of the time, which will drive writers into such a stance.

Here are some distinct factors in the workings of poetry. They are some of the individual grounds for believing that poetry matters.

Pleasure

First of all, poetry gives pleasure. In traditional poetics that function was always coupled, in second place, with instruction: *docere et*

delectare, instruire et plaire, to instruct and to please. But here let's begin
with it. 'A poem,' says Coleridge, 'is that species of composition,
which is opposed to works of science, by proposing for its *immediate*
object pleasure, not truth' (*BL*, 150, 221). Of course, poetry, quite
as much as science, seeks the truth, a different kind of truth; but its
first object is pleasure, as the means to its kind of truth. Very self-
confidently, as though the matter were beyond doubt, Coleridge
calls the object of poetry pleasure and describes its effects as pleasur-
able, a 'pleasurable excitement' (*BL*, 154, 180). Those would be my
terms too, and not in any rarified or narrowly restrictive sense either.
Reading or listening to poetry does indeed excite the mind into
'pleasurable activity' (*BL*, 150), but it quickens the heartbeat and the
pulses too. The experience is sensuous: Keats listening to Chap-
man's Homer, for example. And at a certain line in *Phèdre* Alfred de
Musset fainted clean away. The body participates in the pleasure of
poetry just as the mind (memory, imagination) does in the pleasure
of sex. Dante's lovers Paolo and Francesca are certainly not in hell.
They dwell for ever among the blessed. They are the icon of what
poetry can do to you. The pleasure poetry gives is neither mental
nor physical—if we must use those unhelpful categories—but a mix
of both varying incalculably according to poem, reader, and circum-
stances. People who don't like the idea of poetry giving physical
pleasure are matched, or even outnumbered, by those who don't
want their physical (emotional) pleasure adulterated by any admix-
ture of the mental. These scruples do much harm. Best not to admit
such separation in the first place. 'Thinking,' says Brecht's Galileo,
'is one of the greatest pleasures of the human race.' And Brecht
himself, in the poem 'Vegnügungen' [Pleasures], lists among them,
along with the first look through the window in the morning, swim-
ming, comfortable shoes, and singing, also the act or moment of
understanding [Begreifen], and dialectics.

The pleasure of poetry springs most obviously from the rhythm of
it: that is, from sounds and their more or less definite accentuation
in lines. Poets use metre, says Coleridge, 'for the foreseen purpose
of pleasure' (*BL*, 179). Regular metre was much more customary in
his day than in ours; but all lines of verse, now and then, have a
rhythm, whether metrically constituted and able to be prosodically
described or not. We don't read lines metrically, we feel for their

rhythm and read to that. Rhythm in metrical verse is engendered
by the natural way of saying the line in a 'loving quarrel'[4] with strict
metrical requirement. Rhythm made like that gives pleasure. Leni
Pfeiffer, the engaging (and uneducated) heroine of Heinrich Böll's
novel *Group Portrait with a Lady*, chants her own personal and peculiar
compilation of bits and pieces of Hölderlin's poems, for solace and
delight; and I guess most people would understand her and with
poets of their own might do the same.

But poetry, though it may be musical and may be set and sung,
is never music. Its sounds and rhythms are made of words which
mean something, they are charged with precise lexical sense and,
most often, come trailing centuries of connotations. So the idea that
poetry's object is pleasure, that reading or listening to poetry is
pleasurable, may become problematic if the subject expressed by the
words of a poem is itself unpleasant. To which we have to say that
much, if not most, of the subject matter of poetry is in some sense
'unpleasant'. Absence, sickness, loss, desertion, death are, really,
unpleasant. But poems made of those subjects—a whole anthology
springs to mind!—do beyond doubt give pleasure. Why should that
be? Before trying to answer that question, and agreeing that the
'Ode to Melancholy' and 'Adonais' do indeed give pleasure, let us
ask is it pleasure we get from Owen's 'Dulce et decorum est', these
lines, for example: 'If in some smothering dreams, you too could
pace / Behind the wagon that we flung him in, / And watch the
white eyes writhing in his face, / His hanging face, like a devil's sick
of sin; / If you could hear, at every jolt, the blood / Come gargling
from the froth-corrupted lungs...'? And even worse has been done
since then, that poetry is bound by office to deal with. Adorno was
quite wrong to say (and it is a great pity that his dictum is so often
quoted) that after Auschwitz poetry cannot be written, or that to
write it would be 'barbaric'. It has to be and it can be. Poetry,
unkillable, infinitely inventive, adapts to be able to deal with the
new realities, however vile. You can see it in August Stramm and
Isaac Rosenberg in the First World War, and in Brecht in the
1930s: poets fashioning a poetics to answer the times they live in.
Brecht moved away from rhyme and regular metre (though never
completely) because their use seemed to him not to fit the violently
discrepant realities he must address. He mistrusted the suggestion of

harmony and order that is inherent in rhyme and conventional prosody. (See 'Bad times for lyric poetry': 'a rhyme would seem almost a presumption'.) Celan revoked his own poem about the death camps, 'Todesfuge' [Death Fugue], refusing to let it be reprinted and anthologized. Its incantatory dactyllic metre and fluid weaving of figures and motifs seemed to him, as his poetics progressed, to be engendering a pleasure very out of keeping with the subject matter. Owen understood that risk; which is why, in the preface to the poems he did not live to see published, he sought to root poetry in pity. Like Celan, he knew that the beauty of a poem and the pleasure that beauty gives are never an end in themselves but are that through which a whole complex of effects may be achieved.

The term 'pleasure' in this context requires so much qualification, explanation, and hedging about that some critics have preferred 'satisfaction'. Poetry gives satisfaction. By which is meant (I think) the kind of pleasure you feel when something strikes home, is apt, fitting, perfectly answers a need. Satirical epigrams may have that effect— this by e. e. cummings, for example: 'a politician is an arse upon / which everyone has sat except a man.' Or Hardy's '"Peace upon earth!" was said. We sing it / And pay a million priests to bring it. / After two thousand years of mass / We've got as far as poison-gas.' Or Kipling's: 'If any question why we died, / Tell them, because our fathers lied.'

But let's keep to pleasure. We can get deep into the very nature of poetry, into the good of it, by seeking to understand the pleasure it gives.

Mixed feelings are a human reality. Jaques (in *As You Like It*) is not the only one to *enjoy* melancholy. It is a common experience that sorrow may be sweet. Some have even thought that sorrow in itself is a maker of the beauty of a poem; even: the more sorrowful, the more beautiful. Alfred de Musset, the fainter at the theatre, said (in 'La Nuit de mai'), 'Les plus désespérés sont les chants les plus beaux, / Et j'en sais d'immortels qui sont de purs sanglots' [The most despairing songs are the loveliest / And I know some immortal ones among them that are pure sobs]. In truth poems are not beautiful by virtue of their subject's sadness (or cheerfulness) but by the way the poet shapes that sadness or cheerfulness; which is to say by their form, their words in rhythm. But all we want here for this discussion of pleasure is no more than agreement that in a poem beauty can be made out of feelings that in practical life may be deeply unpleasant. And it is beauty, beautiful form, the whole rhythm of the poem, that gives us pleasure.

In reworking and expanding his *Urfaust* into what he would publish as *Faust, Part I*, Goethe felt obliged to recast into verse some scenes which he had originally written in prose. He commented to Schiller (5 May 1798):

> One very strange thing has come to light in this: some scenes of a tragic nature were written in prose and are now, by their naturalness and power, quite unbearable in relation to the rest. For that reason I am at present trying to cast them into rhyme, for then the idea shines as it were through a veil whilst the effect of the terrible material, previously unmediated, is quietened.

Poetic form, in that understanding, makes the desolating material bearable. Or we might say out of that material, itself 'terrible', 'unbearable', something, a poetic drama, is made which we can, in profound and complex ways, enjoy. That transmutation is as amazing as it is necessary. The *stuff* of tragedy—consider *Oedipus, Lear, Phèdre*—surpasses in horror what most of us would be able to bear; but estranged into poetic form, into dynamic beauty, we, as spectators, as witnesses, enjoy it.

Beauty gives pleasure. Beauty is the form in which truth is brought home to us. The peculiarity of the pleasure that poetic beauty gives us lies in the fact that the truth the poem faces us with may, as fact in real life, be deeply unpleasant, even unbearable. And it may be that truth altogether—the immanent presence of it—is hard to bear, whether the facts-in-life of it are pleasant or unpleasant. The effects that a line of verse may cause a reader or listener to experience, may be indistinguishable as physical effects from those of terror or horror. As Prospero says of Ariel's appearance (as a harpy) before the 'three men of sin': 'a grace it had, devouring'—the beauty of it, the truth it brings home, are consumingly terrible.[5]

Emily Dickinson wrote (in August 1870, to T. W. Higginson): 'If I read a book and it makes my whole body so cold no fire can ever

warm me, I know *that* is poetry.' And here is A. E. Housman, lectur-
ing on the 'The Name and Nature of Poetry':

> Poetry indeed seems to me more physical than intellectual.
> A year or two ago...I received from America a request that
> I would define poetry. I replied that I could no more define
> poetry than a terrier can define a rat, but that I thought we
> both recognized the object by the symptoms which it pro-
> vokes in us...[Then he quotes Job 4:15: 'A spirit passed
> before my face: the hair of my flesh stood up.'] Experience
> has taught me, when I am shaving of a morning, to keep
> watch over my thoughts, because, if a line of poetry strays
> into my memory, my skin bristles so that the razor ceases to
> act. This particular symptom is accompanied by a shiver
> down the spine; there is another which consists in a constric-
> tion of the throat and a precipitation of water to the eyes; and
> there is a third which I can only describe by borrowing a
> phrase from one of Keats's last letters, where he says, speak-
> ing of Fanny Brawne, 'everything that reminds me of her
> goes through me like a spear'. The seat of this sensation is the
> pit of the stomach.[6]

Nothing is said there about the *matter* of the lines of verse causing
those effects. In my experience it may well not be at all definable as
happy, sad, pleasant, or unpleasant, which inclines me to suppose
that the shock the lines give is that of seeing the truth close up, of
feeling it hit home, of being at the mercy of it. Call that pleasure?
In a deep sense, yes. It is akin to, perhaps even the same as, Robert
Graves's 'gratitude for a nightmare': the reconnection of one's life
with what he calls 'solemnities': 'solemnities not easy to withstand'.[7]
We can't live so fully connected all the time; but closed to such visi-
tations, refusing to let them in, life lessens.

It is questionable what *consolation* the active beauty of poems might
or should bring. Owen was insistent that for his generation at least
his poems were, as he said in his Preface, 'in no sense consolatory'.
And few readers or audiences nowadays, I guess, would ask of lyric
poetry or tragedy that it should reconcile us, through catharsis, to
our lot. There is much suffering—man-occasioned—that it would
be quite wrong to be reconciled to. But what beauty and the pleasure

it gives can rightly offer is the hope of what Heaney calls redress. Aestheticism is the pursuit of beauty in art as an end in itself. We want none of that. We want beauty in verse and the pleasure of it as help in answering back, in imagining better, in believing in the possibility of something other than the wrong and ugliness daily being perpetrated. We don't ask for consolation but for quickening by pleasure in beauty to revolt. Poets are makers. Among other things, they make beauty. Beauty thus made is a living affront to all that is ugly in our thinking and in the environment our thinking fashions or allows. Poems give their readers access to beauty, and a life that has had such access is roused and strengthened against ugliness.

Alertness and agility

'Poetry makes nothing happen.'[8] Auden's statement (decoupled from what follows it and abstracted from the poetic context and endlessly trotted out) is wrong on many counts, not least this: that reading or listening to poetry, like all sensuous experience, does things to the brain, does indeed make things happen in the brain. The language of poetry, being inexhaustibly varied, makes an equivalent variety of demands. Much the same might be said about reading or listening to prose perhaps. Reading Kleist in German or Henry James in English is not at all like reading the Gospels in the Luther Bible or in the Authorized Version. Poetry intensifies such difference, which is not just, or even chiefly, one of difficulty. Compare Dryden's heroic couplets in 'Absalom and Achitophel' with Wordsworth's blank verse in *The Prelude*; or that blank verse with Edward Thomas's in 'As the team's head-brass...'; or the compacted, nervous urgency of Emily Dickinson's lines with the headlong skilful pell-mell of C. K. Williams's at their lengthiest. All palpably different when we read; and distinctions just as marked may be felt even within the work of a single poet in his or her deployment of different forms.

Some differences in the reading experience of poetry spring directly from the rules and resources of a particular language's grammar. In German the reading mind will not be surprised by inversions in main clauses; and in subordinate clauses it will expect the postponement of the verb (which means the clinching of sense) to the end. In highly inflected languages like Latin and Greek relations between words, even words that are some distance apart, can be indicated by the inflexions. I suppose that reading a fixed-word-order language like English must cause an activity in the brain very different from that caused by reading or listening to the Australian aboriginal language Warlpiri in which '*This man speared a kangaroo* can be expressed as *Man this kangaroo speared*, *Man kangaroo speared this*, and any of the other four orders, all completely synonymous.'[9] Poetry exploits, extends, bends, and on occasion deliberately breaks the rules of its native language, often working like a translation from a foreign tongue; and a large part of the 'pleasurable excitement' of reading it consists in agilely answering these many demands, promptings, suggestions being flung at you line by line.

Many and various are the modes and kinds of poetry and thus, correspondingly, the ways of reading. A ballad tells a story, and so you move with its lines and verses pretty well chronologically. But some poems—those set out on the page in the shape of their subject (an altar, Easter wings, a bird, a fountain, a bouquet of flowers), such poems and indeed any in the imagist mode—actually subvert chronological reading, so that we apprehend the poem rather as we do a picture, taking in its details if not quite (as in a picture) simultaneously, at least with a sense that we must hold them suspended, co-existent, in play, and that reaching the chronological end, the last sentence's full stop, we may at once begin again, sorting the imagery differently. Indeed in much lyric poetry there is a tension between chronology and simultaneity, most often we are not encouraged (as we are in epigrammatic poetry) to move to a conclusion and have things fall into place. Much lyric poetry resists the onward progress of its lines. Reading goes off laterally, the mind is not permitted to make straight for the end, so much needs entertaining along the way. This lyric *ritardando* is a great beauty and a great virtue of poetry. Here is the first of the three stanzas of Pauline Stainer's 'Afterlight', one of the poems in her collection *Crossing the Snowline* in which she grieves over the death of her daughter and, in so doing, resumes the poetic ability she was deprived of by that death:

> I chose the liquidambar tree
> knowing it would light
> its own dying,
> like those wasted children
> wrapped in gold foil
> to keep them warm.

You can't hurry on, the language does not allow it. Each line, to continue the one sentence, requires the next, but each wants dwelling on. The lovely word *éclosion* comes to mind, a word Ted Hughes was fond of, the hatching, the opening into the imago, the dawning and realization of a feeling, of a sense— those opening lines, like many other entrances into poems, are an *éclosion*.

Ezra Pound, with the help of Basil Bunting, derived the German word for poetry 'Dichtung' from the word 'dicht', meaning 'dense'. The verb 'dichten' then, in his understanding, meant 'to condense': '*dichten* = *condensare*'.[10] His etymologizing is all wrong but, pointing to one possible kind or mode of poetry, he may at least make us alert to texture. Poems have very different textures. They may be more or less dense, limpid, taut, relaxed. And that variety will be matched by our ways of reading. Late Celan—his terribly compressed and fractured verse on the verge of speechlessness—asks for something more like meditation than reading, a meditation on ideograms, closely focusing, possibilities of meaning slowly being engendered. Move from that, to reading the loquacious Whitman. Or from these six lines by Hopkins:

> Not of áll my eyes see, wandering on the world,
> Is anything a milk to the mind so, so sighs deep
> Poetry tó it, as a tree whose boughs break in the sky.
> Say it is ásh-boughs: whether on a December day and furled
> Fast ór they in clammyish lashtender combs creep
> Apart wide and new-nestle at heaven most high...

to these six by W. H. Davies:

> As I walked down the waterside
>   This morning, in the cold damp air,
> I saw a hundred women and men
>   Huddled in rags and sleeping there:

These people have no work, thought I,
And long before their time they die.

Degrees of density, very different textures. Othello, Lear, Macbeth, Antony shift in their speech through an extraordinary scale. Antony, for example, so: 'Fall not a tear, I say; one of them rates / All that is won and lost. Give me a kiss'. Or so: 'The hearts / That spanieled me at heels, to whom I gave / Their wishes, do discandy, melt their sweets / On blossoming Caesar, and this pine is barked / That over-topped them all...' (*Antony and Cleopatra*, 3.11.69–70; 4.12.20–4).

Poetry, extraordinarily various in its ways with words, expects—encourages, trains into being—a matching agility in the reader's mind. The tensing, relaxing, hesitation, suspension, deferral, and resolution that different poems or, even, one poem in itself may deploy as ways and means to the total sense must surely be good exercise for the brain, a flexing, to make it quicker, livelier, more agile. And these effects, which may perhaps be empirically tested and observed, are also suggestive of, and might even be the makers of, a more lasting attitude of mind. At least for the time of reading or listening, and perhaps lastingly thereafter, the mind affected by poetry is open to possibilities, agile in the making of connections, deeply averse to closure.

An alerted, connected, open state of mind is better than one comatose, cut-off, and shut. Poetry can at least help towards the former preferable state. In fact, when poetry works that is what it naturally and always does and may, if let, be a present help towards revolt. A stupefied electorate is at the mercy of those who do the stupefying. No one stupefied can answer back. My English teacher, the one who had the words from Milton's *Areopagitica* on his wall, told us that the purpose of teaching English literature was to increase sales resistance.

Useful and autonomous

I said that we can fairly ask what use poetry is. Bertolt Brecht, in 1927 adjudicating a poetry competition, refused to award the prize because none of the 400 entrants seemed to him to have written anything of any real use. And he asserted: 'lyric poetry especially

ought without doubt to be a thing we must be able to examine for
its usefulness'.[11] Poets who in politically exigent times seek, as poets,
to act upon those times face an unavoidable conflict of the wish to
serve with the need to safeguard poetry's autonomy. Brecht under-
stood that very well; and he expounded theoretically, and in practice
he demonstrated, how best poetry may serve, how most fittingly and
effectively it may make itself useful. Here one instance—almost a
'figurative anecdote'—may at least broach a subject too large for
this context. In August 1940, when Hitler seemed unstoppable,
Brecht, in exile in Finland, was dipping into a volume of Words-
worth's verse, edited by Matthew Arnold, and lit upon 'She was a
Phantom of delight...' It prompted him into some thoughts on how
poetry works, what virtue even such a poem as Wordsworth's ('a
petty-bourgeois idyll'), has, what use it is. He suggested, rather
touchingly, that the Home Guard then patrolling England's fields
with their 'shotguns and Molotov cocktails', might be reminded by
'A lovely Apparition, sent / To be a moment's ornament' of situa-
tions more worthy of human beings. That is, the poem, written in
1804 but making no reference at all to the Revolutionary Wars,
might by its very self, as poem, act in 1940 like a charge of energy
and hope among people in very desperate circumstances. And
Brecht passed from that suggestion to this—not easy—dictum: 'Art
is an autonomous, though never under any circumstances an autar-
kic, zone.'[12] By 'autonomous', concerning poetry, is meant that it
operates according to laws and conventions and by means which are
peculiarly its own. And it must safeguard that autonomy. At the
same time it can never be 'autarkic'—that is, never self-sufficient;
and for the obvious reason, that it lives in the midst of human life
and must import all its material, with which then it works autono-
mously, from that life.

   In all poets seeking to act upon or be close and truthful witnesses
to the times they are living in, this conflict between the desire to
serve and the need for autonomy will always be more or less pain-
fully manifest. The more definitely *engagés* among them do some-
times risk or forfeit their proper autonomy; which means that in
their great oeuvre there are failures, writings in which poetry has
not held its own against the too explicit demands of the cause.
Amply made up for elsewhere, these failures are part of the cost,

and worth it. Brecht, Neruda, Darwish are so thoroughly poets that they demonstrate abundantly what poetry—it alone, it in its unique way—can do to oppose the evil and serve the good in the midst of the real world's often terrible exigencies. Our war poets, Owen, Rosenberg, Douglas, and the many others; Russia's poet-heroes and poet-witnesses, Mandelstam, Akhmatova, Tsvetayeva, Pasternak, all assert the value of being human. Constantly, as Brecht puts it, they remind us of 'situations more worthy of human beings', and they do so by the main force, by the peculiar and irrepressible will-to-live of their lyric poetry. They were themselves *en situation*, and could not get out of it. Miłosz, Heaney, and others defended the autonomy of their art by removing themselves from the immedate zone of the conflict and by refusing to be made the champions of a cause, how-ever just. All Heaney's long meditation on the redress that poetry can effect, springs from that removing himself to a distance (still close), the better to safeguard the autonomy of poetry and to exploit its powers. This loyalty, which is itself a loyalty to a very demanding cause, *costs*. Graham Greene said 'there is a splinter of ice in the heart of every writer'. There's a bit, and more than a bit, of bad conscience in every writer too. Knowing the pleasure that writing gives, knowing that when they are writing they are doing what they deeply want to do, how can they in good conscience turn aside, to write, from lives having no such satisfaction and in need of immedi-ate help?

Wilfred Owen was awarded the Miltary Cross 'for conspicuous gallantry and devotion to duty in the attack on the Fonsomme Line on 1st/2nd October 1918'. He wrote to his mother after that battle: 'I came out in order to help these boys—directly by leading them as well as an officer can; indirectly, by watching their sufferings that I may speak of them as well as a pleader can. I have done the first.' He was killed on 4 November, helping his men of the 2nd Manches-ters fix duckboards and planks, to get across the Sambre and Oise canal. He went to and fro among them, patting them on the back and saying, 'Well done!' and 'You are doing very well, my boy.' As poet he had watched their sufferings, spoken of them, pleaded. Another word he uses for that act of witness is 'warn'. In his Preface he wrote, 'All a poet can do today is warn. That is why the true Poets must be truthful.'

On 1 April 1957 Anna Akhmatova added this prefatory note to her poem 'Requiem' (written 1935–43):

> In the terrible years of the Ezhov purges I spent seventeen months in the queues outside the prison in Leningrad. It happened that one day someone 'recognised' me. And then the woman with blue lips who was standing behind me, who of course had never in her life heard my name, woke from the stupor which was common to us all, and spoke in my ear (we all whispered there): 'This, can you describe this?' And I said, 'Yes, I can'. Then something much like a smile slipped across what had once been her face.

And in 1961, above that note, she placed this epigraph:

> No, not under a foreign sky,
> Nor in the shelter of a foreign wing,
> With my people, there stood I
> With them, in their suffering.
>
> (Translated by Sasha Dugdale)

The poem, being in the midst of and drawing on the stuff of common life and therefore never self-sufficient, is a locus in which a free play of possibilities is not only permitted but required. Without that freedom no poem can be written. With it, a thing can be made which will excite in its reader a freedom akin to that enjoyed by the poet in its making. Many thinkers and—whether they articulated it or not—all poets of the Romantic Age were haunted by the unfreedom lurking in some contemporary understandings of the working of the human mind. The materialist and determinist theories of Locke, Hume, and Hartley seemed to risk reducing the mind, or the human person altogether, to a mechanism. Coleridge's raising the 'esemplastic power' of Imagination above the merely 'aggregative and associative power' of Fancy is one such bid for freedom against the threat of enslavement into mechanics. The same anxiety haunts Hölderlin's poetics: the horror of *Maschinengang* [mechanical process].[13] It scarcely needs saying that the context of such fears, was then, was before then, and is still the manifest unfreedom of most people under the social order. So poets like Hölderlin and Blake, writing in times of deep and wide oppression, presented to a readership—largely nonexistent in the case of the former, very small in the case of the lat-ter—a feeling of what freedom of the imagination *and* in social living would be like. And they did so in poems.

Unfreedom is a chief characteristic of our times. The markets oper-ate beyond the command and even beyond the ken of those suppos-edly managing them. The actual unfreedom of the citizens increases, it often seems, in direct proportion to their being offered 'choice'. For many, real options are being systematically closed down. There is less and less social mobility; which is to say that many in our society, not just the jobless, also those indentured to menial and badly paid labour, have nowhere to go. In our global economy many, perhaps most, citi-zens have for a long time lived in the conviction that beyond their immediate locality no good can be done. And now their locality is also being degraded by powers which locally elected councillors are not able (not free) to oppose. The financiers, the captains of industry, the chief executive officers, still rich, still getting richer, have no local-ity; they belong nowhere, they will always relocate to wherever yet more money can be made most easily. But their mobility is an enslave-ment too. Existentially, they are in hell; which may be why they refer to their bonuses as 'compensations'. The indentured poor, unable to move, are matched by the rich who are free to move only to another gated community, living there among their own kind, fearful, on the treadmill of making nothing but more money.

Unfreedom is a chief characteristic of our thinking. Our thinking has to change, has to be always capable of changing. A set mind is a dangerous thing (far more dangerous than a little learning). Our present mindset is lethal.

Poetry now, every bit as much as in the Romantic Age, is a uto-pian demonstration, by aesthetic means, of what true freedom would be like. It engages us to imagine something better than what at present we are afflicted with; it helps keep hope alive; it incites us to make more radical demands. And poetry does that out of the enjoy-ment of its own autonomy, which it is duty-bound not to forfeit.

Having or being

It is an ancient distinction, having or being, and by many thinkers the latter state or way has been thought much the better. I first read

Erich Fromm more than thirty years ago. A student lent me his copy—the book must have just come out—I can't remember his name, I don't think he was even one of my academic pupils, but he came to see me and lent me *To Have or to Be?*, because, he said, he wanted to know what I would make of it. And now I am reading the book again, it fits my needs, and I am touched, as I was more than thirty years ago, that a student wanted to know what I would make of it.

Poetry, for writer and reader, sides decisively with being. Poetry cannot be had. Saying that, I am very aware that in schools and universities it is often taught (with exams in mind) as though it can indeed and must at all costs be had. In that view, whether explicitly stated or not, all the workings of a poem serve to produce a thing called 'the meaning', which the clever reader will get and take away. The whole poem, in that understanding of it, is a means to an end: a meaning; and once that meaning has been had, the poem itself may be dispensed with. There is a kind of language which rightly and properly may be used for such a purpose, which subordinates itself to the message, the facts, the instructions it conveys and once having served in that way its job is done. But poetry—and this is not a value judgement, only a distinguishing of function—does not work like that. Intrinsically, it resists being instrumentalized, except in the sense that all its parts work together for the purpose of pleasurable realization, which is itself a process not of acquiring but of becoming: of coming into a state of enhanced being. Reading acquisitively, in an anxious effort to gut the poem of its 'meaning' so as to carry that meaning away with you, such reading shuts you, the reader, against the poem's peculiar virtue. Eliot describes the state or disposition most favourable to the writing of poetry as a 'passive attending upon the event',[14] and we can say: most favourable to the reading of poetry also—patient, watchful, open, both waiting for and an assistant at the realization, the event. Not grasping, not anxiously seeking to possess.

Robet Lowell said, 'A poem is an event, not the record of an event.'[15] Applied in this context, and with the quotation from Eliot's essay in mind, Lowell's dictum should help us understand that the poem for the writer and for the reader is a present experience. In a very real sense all poems, even those recollecting past or imagining future experience, move only in the present tense. They are happening now in whoever is reading them. Nietzsche called the Kingdom of Heaven 'ein Zustand des Herzens' [a state of the heart],[16] and that may be said of the poem too as it works in the reader: present, earthly, incarnated in a living person. Auden, having said that 'poetry makes nothing happen'—I disagree—says then that it is 'a way of happening', which hits very exactly the present and dynamic experience of reading a poem. This presentness is, I should say, what Elizabeth Bishop felt in Hopkins's rhythms when (in an undergraduate essay!) she remarked that they were the vehicle not of thoughts but of 'a mind thinking'.[17]

Just after the First World War Lawrence wrote an essay called 'Poetry of the Present'. We need, he says there, a poetry that will address the *terra incognita* (his word) of the present, of now, of the instant. The sentences themselves give the feeling of what is wanted:

> But there is another kind of poetry: the poetry of that which is at hand: the immediate present. In the immediate present there is no perfection, no consummation, nothing finished. The strands are all flying, quivering, intermingling into the web, the waters are shaking the moon. There is no round, consummate moon on the face of running water, nor on the face of the unfinished tide...
>
> Life, the ever-present, knows no finality, no finished crystal-lisation. The perfect rose is only a running flame, emerging and flowing off, and never in any sense at rest, static, finished. Herein lies its transcendent loveliness. The whole tide of all life and all time suddenly heaves, and appears before us as an apparition, a revelation. We look at the very white quick of nascent creation...
>
> There is poetry of this immediate present, instant poetry, as well as poetry of the infinite past and the infinite future. The seething poetry of the incarnate Now is supreme, beyond even the everlasting gems of the before and after. In its quivering momentaneity it surpasses the crystalline pearl-hard jewels, the poems of the eternities. Do not ask for the qualities of the

unfading timeless gems. Ask for the whiteness which is the seethe of mud, ask for that incipient putrescence which is the skies falling, ask for the never-pausing, never-ceasing life itself. There must be mutation, swifter than iridescence, haste, not rest, come-and-go, not fixity, inconclusiveness, immediacy, the quality of life itself, without denouement or close. There must be the rapid momentaneous association of things which meet and pass on the for ever incalculable journey of creation: everything left in its own rapid, fluid relationship with the rest of things.

The first poet waking wholly to the present, says Lawrence, was Whitman. 'This is the unrestful, ungraspable poetry of the sheer present, poetry whose very permanency lies in its wind-like transit. Whitman's is the best poetry of this kind. Without beginning and without end, without any base and pediment, it sweeps past for ever, like a wind that is for ever in passage, and unchainable.... He is so near the quick.'[18]

'Poetry of the Present' (1919), intended as a preface to Lawrence's collection *Look! We have come through!*, actually served to introduce his *New Poems* in America in 1920. But the fullest realization of the poetics came in *Birds, Beasts and Flowers* (1923). Several of the poems in that volume return to the same subject: fig-trees and figs; almond trees; bats; tortoises; goats. And within any single poem there is a good deal of quite deliberate coming again and again at an essentially elusive centre; never an exact repetition, rather a trying again, a rephrasing and modification in the bid to come closer. In 'Sicilian Cyclamens', for example, he approaches the flowers through images of them first as toads, then as greyhounds, then as hares. And it is not that one image replaces another, as being more apt. None quite lapses, all remain possible, the effect is cumulative. I should have to quote the whole poem to illustrate this adequately. But here are the greyhounds, still harking back to the toads ('out of earth', 'stone-engendered') and anticipating their quarry, the hares:

> The shaking aspect of the sea
> And man's defenceless bare face
> And cyclamens putting their ears back.
> Long, pensive, slim-muzzled greyhound buds

Dreamy, not yet present,
Drawn out of earth
At his toes.

Dawn-rose
Sub-delighted, stone-engendered
Cyclamens, young cyclamens
Arching
Waking, pricking their ears
Like delicate very-young greyhound bitches
Half-yawning at the open, inexperienced
Vista of day,
Folding back their soundless petalled ears.

Greyhound bitches
Bending their rosy muzzles pensive down,
And breathing soft, unwilling to wake to the new day
Yet sub-delighted.

The effect of this strategy (it *is* a strategy) is to make the subject feel inexhaustible and essentially intractable. All that metamorphosis, and still it needs more! Failure itself points up the excess of the living subject over the poet's powers. Of course, we have to be persuaded that the poet *has* powers. Incompetence will not show up the elusive quickness of the subject, only the writer's incompetence. But since Lawrence at his best is very good indeed, the sense he excites in us that the subject exceeds even him, is a mark of his success in doing it justice.

Life exceeds art and the best poets write in such a way as to—joyfully, gratefully—demonstrate that fact.

It helps in the re-reading of a poem you are familiar with, if you can clear your mind of what you thought about it last time. Hardly anything is more hampering in the fresh enjoyment of a poem than trying to remember what you thought 'it meant' when you read it before. Altogether, now that we can store and instantly access an infinite amount of information, forgetting may be an ability poet and reader equally should cultivate. Remembering, allowing yourself to be reminded of, what you think you know already, rarely helps in the writing and reading of poetry. Most often it will only harm. The chief reason for not revealing, until the exercise is over, the author or date of a poem offered for close reading and practical criticism is that readers possessed of either bit of information will easily tip what they can remember about either the poet or his or her times on to the poem in advance of actually reading it. Then in the murk they can't see the thing itself. What Nietzsche called contemptuously 'reines Wissen um' [mere knowledge about],[19] may often, since it is something we *have*, hinder us on the way to *being*.

Reading needs to match the thing being read. The poem's demands and opportunities are quite peculiar. First and foremost perhaps, the poem requires us and, if we let it, will help us, to be. We can't own (possess) a poem. But we can make a poem 'our own' by ingesting it, changingly, into how we live. In Rilke's sonnet 'Archaic Torso of Apollo', the reader is confronted, through the poem, by the battered remnant of a work of art and looked at by its every sparkling pore. All its force has been contracted into what remains, particularly into the loins, the generative parts. The statue-poem itself, in its last half-line, issues this admonition: 'du musst dein Leben ändern' [you must change your life].

The lethal mindset I referred to earlier is, of course, barren of any suggestion that you should live differently. Its murderousness consists precisely in urging you to carry on as usual: have, have more, consume, get more and more. Which is to say it marshals you the way that you were going, further and further along the way of having, which is the way of death.

Silence, the space, returns, immanence, face to face

It happens again and again that you read angry laments about the state of things—Blake or Hölderlin on soulless labour, Clare on Enclosure ('Fence meeting fence in owner's little bounds'[20])—and you think: even then it was a thing it lacerated them to witness. And you think: much that we live with would be, to them, a horror beyond all nightmare. Aldous Huxley, in his *Perennial Philosophy*, which is a commentated anthology of writings on the religiously grounded life, observes in the chapter 'Silence':

> The twentieth century is, among other things, the Age of Noise. Physical noise, mental noise and noise of desire – we

hold history's record for all of them. And no wonder; for all the resources of our almost miraculous technology have been thrown into the current assault against silence.

And of advertising ('the organized effort to extend and intensify craving') he says that it 'has but one purpose—to prevent the will from ever achieving silence'.[21] His book was published in 1946, since when the noise has got ubiquitously worse: louder, more insistent, more penetrative, annihilating for many all memory of, all desire for, silence. A part of this noise is fed directly into the head—the head which, even without that contribution, is at the mercy of ear-worms and an abundance of other mithering bits and pieces, some worded, some more like a white noise of anger, anxiety, inanity, and panic. Silence don't come easy.

Writers complain about being continually interrupted—but work with email on, waiting for the next ping. One successful novelist told me not in the least shamefacedly that he kept his Amazon rating minimized but visible on the screen, alert to its every up or down, watchful, perhaps, for the best moment to sell shares in himself. But Ted Hughes covered the windows of his Boston flat with brown paper, and wore earplugs, to isolate himself from all distraction. And lifelong (so I have been told) his maxim was: 'Not being interrupted is good. Better is knowing you *can't* be interrupted.' Graves worked at poems in a trance, wishing to hear no sound but that of the lines taking shape. Lines like this, for example: 'In a deep thought of you and concentration...'

In Kafka's story 'Josefine die Sängerin oder Das Volk der Mäuse' [Josephine the Singer or The Tribe of Mice], the narrator doubts whether what Josefine 'does' is singing at all, or whether it isn't what any of the tribe might do: just a whistling, and in her case a rather feeble whistling at that. But he concedes that her activity, whatever its nature, has a valuable effect: it makes a pause and a space for silence in the anxious and hurrying lives of the tribe. They obey her bossy insistence that what she does matters. She causes them to halt, they bow their heads and listen. Or perhaps they don't really listen. But in the midst of fret and danger they bow their heads and are silent for the duration of her performance.

Poetry, if let, will make such a pause and space. Not quite so bossily as Josefine, it asks to be given a proper hearing. In earlier traditions, as I have already mentioned, this claim on a reader's or listener's attention was very forceful. Pindar's Victory Odes, for example, were performed by a chorus, delivered to music, probably in something like recitative, and their complex metrical responsions were reinforced by dance, or at least a measured walking in time one way during the recitation of the strophe, back again during the antistrophe, and for the epode standing still. (Ben Jonson's terms for that procedure are 'Turne', Counter-Turne', and 'Stand'.) The metres, the difficult, often archaic, language, the performance, were the signals that something beneficially strange was being offered, and should be heeded. In the West at least poetry has for a long time been chary of presenting itself so commandingly. But always it has by one means or another signalled its peculiarity; and so, always and still, it must.

Waking the other night at the bad time when the mind turns to self-torment, I countered by remembering first lines of poems, the poem's first bid for your particular attention. How arresting, shocking, intriguing, inviting, compelling so many of them are! Titles may be helpful, often indeed they are necessary, but it is a poem's first line that hooks you. It may alert you at once to a characteristic stance and tone of voice. In two volumes of John Clare's poems edited by Robinson and Powell, twenty-eight open with the words 'I love' or 'I loved', a typical whole line being 'I love Primroses wi their mole eyed faces'. Many poems, by ancient and modern poets alike, have an addressee, which in practice, listening or reading, is you. So the poem may come at you roughly—'Natures lay Ideot, I taught thee to love…' or with a savage grief: 'Cold in the earth, and the deep snow piled above thee!' You may be male or female, living or dead. Or you might be a Greek vase, a bird, a god or a goddess, a mouse, the moon, a field-gun, the poem may suddenly address you in any conceivable shape or form. Adjust, and pay *double* attention! For of course, you are both speaker and spoken to. It is striking how often an opening line defers its grammatical subject: 'Women he liked, did shovel-bearded Bob…' Or sets up a grammatical construction which it will take some lines—'Let the world's sharpness like a clasping knife…', or the whole poem,'When

I have fears that I may cease to be...'—to conclude. Or they open on a comparison and you must wait to touch the thing itself: 'As an unperfect actor on the stage...' These deferrals are to engage you on something it will be worth your while continuing with. Another strategy is to usher you into a fluid situation: 'And if tonight my soul may find her peace...'[22] And akin to that, if the poem is to rhyme, or to proceed with a refrain, moving through stanzas, the first line, feeling its way, begins a shape which will then, as you read or listen, be established and go on its determined course, bearing you with it. So the first line of a ghazal ends with the *radif*, the word or phrase that will sound in that position through the whole poem: 'When you wake to jitters every day, it's heartache...' Seven times: 'it's heartache.'[23] A villanelle opens with the line out of which, by ingenious turnings, the whole advancing poem must be spun. In Elizabeth Bishop's 'One Art' that opening—'The art of losing isn't hard to master' —is an assertion, almost a precept, that in the eighteen following lines she will mull over, with a poignancy even greater than her cleverness, so that, closing the form, she has opened the initial statement to a variety of feelings and reflections.

Devised in these ways and in many others, a poem's first line (whether or not it was the first composed) is the signal that something is beginning that concerns you. You are being asked to make, as the poem itself does, 'a new effort of attention'.[24] The opening line is your admission into the space, the pause, the silence of concentration that is the reading or the listening to the poem. And for the poet it is in a kindred space, pause, and silence that the poem later to be read or listened to first materializes. A blank page is a dizzying thing. You might begin to write for no better reason than that blankness is unbearable. But writing, you consequentially reduce the possibilities inherent in the emptiness. Which is why you hold off as long as possible. You know very well that the words you set down may not be on the way towards but *in the way of* the poem. They may actually make it less likely that you will ever get where you feel you want to be.

Realizing, materializing, embodying, incarnating: many of the words we might reach for to describe what happens when a poem is made have religious connotations; and some poets whose concerns can fairly be called religious (in any named faith or none) have understood the making of a poem not just as an image of the working of divine presence but as the very bodily experience of it or, even more boldly, the means by which that devoutly wished for consummation might be induced to happen. In practice, if we remember also how *present* the reader's experience in such poems is, the distinctions between 'mere' image of immanence, the thing itself, and the means to that thing, may be unenforceable. And nor will it do, as far as felt truth is concerned, to rate one sort of absence and presence above another. The draining away of all sense out of life, the loss of joy, the condition of dejection, may be experienced by the atheist every bit as keenly as by the believing and doubting Christian; likewise the returns, the joyous resurrections. Herbert, Coleridge, Hölderlin, Hopkins, R. S. Thomas, whatever their particular religious and secular affiliations, really are, in certain of their poems, on common ground, as any reader fearing or knowing absence and wanting presence will recognize. No poem is disposed to be all things to all men; but, rooted in common humanity, poetry is by its very nature generous in the access it allows. For adolescents so convinced of their own worthlessness they cut themselves, I have more than once written out in capital letters Hopkins's 'MY OWN HEART LET ME MORE HAVE PITY ON'.

Nobody in the condition of dejection can write about it. Coleridge could write his ode on the subject only when the 'shaping spirit of imagination' had returned to him. In that one poem he found the words in rhythm to incarnate first what dejection and then what release, enlivening, the return of joy, feel like. There is another such return in George Herbert's poem 'The Flower'. He writes:

> How fresh, O Lord, how sweet and clean
> Are thy returns! ev'n as the flowers in spring;
> To which, besides their own demean,
> The late-past frosts tributes of pleasure bring.
> Grief melts away
> Like snow in May,
> As if there were no such cold thing.
>
> Who would have thought my shrivel'd heart
> Could have recover'd greenness? It was gone
> Quite underground...

> And now in age I bud again,
> After so many deaths I live and write;
> I once more smell the dew and rain,
> And relish versing...

Herbert was a country parson of the Church of England and, clearly, the return his poem celebrates is the return of the presence of the God he believes in into his life. But on that inrush, as the felt truth of it, comes the renewed ability to savour the earth and to 'relish versing'; which I take to mean, since he is a poet as well as a parson, the ability to write. Such a return is the answer to the prayer uttered again and again by Hopkins: 'Mine, O thou lord of life, send my roots rain.'

The writing of a poem is proof that the gift has returned. It is the gift in practice, the event. But very often that return is used to depict not presence, immanence, fulfilment, but absence, the hope. There are only moments of immanence, at most short passages of it, in Hölderlin's poetry. In the years immediately prior to his mind's collapse he seems to have lived in the frequent, indeed almost steady, possession of his gift. And to have put it to conveying what absence, loss, the hope of recovery feels like. He makes poems which are a preparation for fulfilment, a house for the coming in of it. The quite peculiar poignancy and excitement of his verse lies precisely there: in his making ready, in the waiting, in hope rising on the lines to a crest of imminence, and in the fact, made palpable in supremely successful poetry, of continual disappointment. And for moments, for brief passages, he will make palpable what fulfilment feels like, what it *would* feel like in life. That achievement in verse drives the poem on to desire it really in life. He wrote his 'Friedensfeier' [Celebration of Peace] in the fervent hope that the Peace of Lunéville (1801) would realize the ideals let loose on the world by the revolutions of 1776 and 1789. The long opening sentence, actually putting in place only the setting, structure, furniture of the locus of fulfilment, feels in its rhythm, in its deferment of a conclusion, like the incoming of the ideal itself. When it ends—on 'the tables rise'—a place has been prepared, and the building of it, the making of it in verse, has felt like the coming in of the desired body and spirit whose house this was to be.

> Aired through and with the heavens'
> Still echoing, still peaceably proceeding
> Harmonies stands the ancient
> Sweetly familiar hall, joy drifts in fragrances
> Over the cloths of green and laden
> With ripest fruits and gold-wreathed chalices
> Over the levelled ground, this side and that in a long
> Well-ordered splendid shining
> The tables rise. For here
> At this hour of evening
> From distant places a loving company
> Is called to meet.

In the poetry of R. S. Thomas, uncertain priest that he was, the most characteristic gesture is, as in Hölderlin's, watching and waiting. The construction of the poem 'In Church' and 'Kneeling', its syntax, the rhythms of its lines, is, like the church itself, a structure into which, he devoutly hopes, a real presence may be induced to enter. Church and syntax are the house of an absent god. The act of verse, which in this case at least is akin to the act of prayer, is, he hopes, the means to immanence. But really what is made present is 'only' the desire for immanence. The bones want flesh, blood, a living life. That life, in such poems, consists in longing.

> Often I try
> To analyse the quality
> Of its silences. Is this where God hides
> From my searching? I have stopped to listen,
> After the few people have gone,
> To the air recomposing itself
> For vigil. It has waited like this
> Since the stones grouped themselves about it.
> These are the hard ribs
> Of a body that our prayers have failed
> To animate. Shadows advance
> From their corners to take possession
> Of places the light held
> For an hour. The bats resume
> Their business. The uneasiness of the pews
> Ceases. There is no other sound
> In the darkness but the sound of a man

> Breathing, testing his faith
> On emptiness, nailing his questions
> One by one to an untenanted cross.

The poem is itself 'the sound of a man / breathing'; and breathing is proof of life and, as breathing into, inspiriting, it is the making of life.

Face to face

Since divine immanence may not be everybody's cup of tea, I must enlarge the idea that poetry is a locus of, even a means to, presence, so that we see those workings, the good they do, in more immediately secular and social ways. When Goethe published his 'Roman Elegies' in 1795 he omitted four which, he knew, would give particular offence. In the second of them the lover is undressing the girl and carrying her to bed:

> Näher haben wir das! Schon fällt dein wollenes Kleidchen,
> So wie der Freund es gelöst, faltig zum Boden hinab.
> Eilet trägt er das Kind, in leichter linnener Hülle,
> Wie es der Amme geziemt, scherzend aufs Lager hinan.

[Now we are nearer, already your lover undoing it / Down slips your woollen dress in folds to the floor. / Nursing you in his arms, sheathed only lightly in linen, / Girl in a laughing hurry he carries you to the bed.]

Much of the virtue of poetry is contained in those first four words whose literal sense is 'nearer we have it' but which in the context—the girl already mostly undressed and the bed step by step closer—might be amplified so: 'Now we are getting somewhere, now we are nearer the real thing in its unique self and truth.' Arriving, they enjoy 'die Freuden des echten nacketen Amors' [Amor's true naked delights]. Poetry brings things close.

It might bring them *very* close, into an intensity of being and of confronting us that we should find hard to bear. That is how children face things in Graves's poem 'The Cool Web':

> Children are dumb to say how hot the day is,
> How hot the scent is of the summer rose,

> How dreadful the black wastes of evening sky,
> How dreadful the tall soldiers drumming by.

Adults are protected:

> But we have speech, to chill the angry day,
> And speech, to dull the rose's cruel scent.
> We spell away the overhanging night,
> We spell away the soldiers and the fright.

Protected by the 'cool web of language', we retreat 'from too much joy or too much fear'. I said earlier that in the Classical tradition poetry was understood as the clothing of a subject (*res*) in words (*verba*); but in practice, and in Romantic poetics, the successful poem, like the lover in Goethe's elegy, divests the subject of its customary garment, so that we see it bare. Then it is like the shock Troilus gets when Cressida first unveils herself to him: 'You have bereft me of all words, lady' (*Troilus and Cressida*, 3.2.53). Her unveiling, his speechlessness, is a good image of how poetry, employing words, can return us to something like a non-verbal or pre-verbal sense of things, into at least a memory of being face to face with unmediated life.

I saw a benign version of this (though it had, itself, nothing to do with poetry) in my father when he came home, still speechless, out of hospital after a stroke. Seeing him in his garden, an obsolete word swam up in me, the word 'seely'. In its kindest senses—happy, blissful, blessed, holy, innocent—it reached into Shakespeare's day, and was survived after that by the word 'silly', whose chief modern sense is foolish or feeble-minded. My father was, I thought, seeing things without the words interposing themselves between them and him. And I looked for words to say what that was like:

Aphasia

He never said much. Less and less in there.
Till nothing. 'But he squoze my hand,' she said,
'And at least he smiled.' His smile! There used to be
A word for it in the childhood of the tongue
The word 'seely' that came up from the roots
And died but left a ghostly twin, a word
That shifts among the grown-ups still, the word 'silly'.

The stuck for words, I've watched them hit the place
The word should be and find it gone and claw
The air for it and pluck the sheet and close
Their eyes and groan, knowing it's nowhere near
The tip of the tongue but on a piece of once
And no longer terra firma come adrift
Somewhere arctic going mushy in a fog.

Not him. Not then. Come home from being in
Without a word he viewed the garden like
Someone let off, someone let in to where
The things divest. Seely the face
That looks like that, seely the smile on her
Whose talk was lovely rapid like a nymph's become a stream's,
Seely the two in silence like before they knew their names.

I said earlier that you can learn what poetry is through what it isn't. A good text for that negative way to knowledge would be Zygmunt Bauman's *Modernity and the Holocaust*. Bauman argues that the Holocaust was made feasible by the conditions of our modernity; not only by our technology—the railway lines, the gas, the efficient crematoria—but also and even more by the cast and habits of mind induced and reinforced by the modern state. The 'Entfernung' [literally 'distancing'] of the Jews was presented to the bureaucracy of Nazi Germany as a problem capable of being solved in a bureaucratic way; and they duly solved it, as they would any other capable of being solved by the minds and the means that an efficient modern bureaucracy disposes of. There are no grounds for believing that the murderers of six million Jews were mostly abnormal people. They were not. It has been shown that perhaps only one in ten even of the SS were unusually cruel, or deranged. The other ninety per cent were ordinary citizens doing their job. They were able to because they were operating in a system which authorized them to do that job and made it routine. As Hannah Arendt observed, one element in the whole 'problem' of exterminating an entire race was 'how to overcome...the animal pity by which all normal men are affected in the presence of physical suffering'.[25] The system achieved just that, by distancing the operators from the ultimate consequences of their little decisions and their little acts, and by instilling in them, to the exclusion of any other ethic, the bureaucrat's own: loyalty to the job, satisfaction in doing it well. 'Only disconnect' is the effective motto of such a bureaucracy: actions from morality, people from their natural pity.

In a notorious experiment conducted in the early 1960s the American psychologist Stanley Milgram found that he could induce two-thirds of his subjects to inflict (as they believed) very severe electric shocks on a fellow human being merely by authorizing them to do so, by telling them it was in the interests of science. Thirty per cent were willing to continue to the very end if they were told to force the victim's hand on to the plate through which the shock was supposedly being administered; forty per cent would do it if sat at a control desk and told to manipulate levers. When the victim was hidden, but his screams were still audible, the number of subjects ready to see it through jumped to sixty-two and a half per cent. Switching off the sound pushed the percentage up to sixty-five. Further, Milgram reported, 'When the subject was not ordered to push the trigger that shocked the victim, but merely to perform a subsidiary act…before another subject actually delivered the shock…thirty-seven out of forty adults…continued to the highest shock level'—which on the control desk was marked 'Very Dangerous'.[26]

The point is obvious: human beings are wondrously capable of doing as they're told; and by a system that distances them from a proper appreciation of the consequences of their acts, that capacity is greatly increased.

Bauman cites and expounds with approval Emmanuel Levinas's view that our primary existential state as human beings is responsibility. 'Being with others', that is being in the world with any other human being, is a state of unconditional responsibility. Responsibility comes from proximity, from the fact of being near, from the first sight of the face of a fellow human being. Levinas says, 'The face orders and ordains me.'[27] Our responsibility—this is the application of Levinas's teaching to the workings of the bureaucratic state—will be eroded and in the end eradicated if we can be distanced and disconnected from one another. Bureaucracy and the technology it commands will by their very nature, if we let them, do precisely that. The order of a modern society is thus subversive of, and will in the end (if we let it) be lethal to, our instinctive way of being with others. As we live and are managed now we are essentially at risk.

Poetry won't stop the worst things happening. Against the always potentially lethal structures and mindset of a bureaucracy and a technology released from ethical control nothing will help except the politics of a sceptical, critical, and eternally vigilant pluralism. But in the urgent business of fetching things so close that we are bound to see them, of particularizing, naming, keeping things real and concrete, of making sure that the human being always has a face—in that very necessary undertaking, poetry will help.[28]

Notes

1. George Seferis, *Days of 1945–51: A Poet's Journal* (Cambridge, Mass.: Belknap Press of Harvard University Press, 1974), 134.
2. Jeanette Winterson, *Why Be Happy When You Could Be Normal?* (London: Vintage, 2011), 40. And see also, even more powerfully and poignantly expressed, the same need for poetry in Andrea Ashworth, *Once in a House on Fire* (London: Picador, 1999), 225, 259, 267, for example.
3. Lines from Brecht's poem 'An die Nachgeborenen' [To those coming after]. On Schiller and Hölderlin in Frankfurt, see my *Hölderlin* (Oxford: Clarendon Press, 1988), 60 and 80–1.
4. I have taken the phrase—in German: 'in liebendem Streit'—from Hölderlin's poem 'An Diotima' (I, 210).
5. *The Tempest*, 3.3.53, 84. And see also Rilke, *Duino Elegies*, I, ll. 4–5: 'Denn das Schöne ist nichts / als des Schrecklichen Anfang' [For beauty is nothing / but the start of terror].
6. A. E. Housman, *The Name and Nature of Poetry* (Cambridge: Cambridge University Press, 1933), 46–7.
7. Graves, 'Gratitude for a Nightmare' and 'A Love Story'.
8. W. H. Auden, 'In Memory of W. B. Yeats', Part II: 'For poetry makes nothing happen:…it survives, / A way of happening, a mouth.'
9. Stephen Pinker, *The Language Instinct* (London: Penguin Books, 1994), 232.
10. Ezra Pound, *The ABC of Reading* (1934; rpt. New York: New Directions, 1960), 34.
11. Bertolt Brecht, *Über Lyrik* (Frankfurt: Suhrkamp, 1968), 8.
12. Brecht, *Über Lyrik*, 72 (from a diary entry 24 August 1940). See *OED*, for 'autonomous': 'Of a subject or discipline: conforming to its own laws and principles which are not simply deducible from or reducible to those of a more fundamental subject; existing independently of other subjects.' And for 'autarky', the quotation from T. S. Eliot's *On Poetry & Poets* (London: Faber and Faber, 1957): 'A general *autarky* in culture simply will not work: the hope of perpetuating the culture of any country lies in communication with others.'
13. Hölderlin, IV, 278. Similarly in Coleridge (*BL*, 57, 97, 190) the horror of 'blind mechanism', 'cold mechanism', 'mechanical art'.
14. In 'Tradition and the Individual Talent', *Selected Prose of T. S. Eliot*, ed. Frank Kermode (London: Faber and Faber, 1975), 43.

15. Robert Lowell, *Interviews and Memoirs* (Ann Arbor, Mich.: University of Michigan Press, 1988), 304.

16. Nietzsche, 'Der Antichrist', section 34, in *Werke*, III, 642–3.

17. Elizabeth Bishop, 'Gerard Manley Hopkins: Notes on Timing in his Poetry', in *Vassar Review*, 1934. Also in *Elizabeth Bishop: Poems, Prose and Letters*, ed. Robert Giroux and Lloyd Schwartz (New York: Farrar, Straus and Giroux, 2008).

18. D. H. Lawrence, *Selected Literary Criticism*, ed. Anthony Beal (London: Mercury Books, 1961), 85–7.

19. Nietzsche, 'Vom Nutzen und Nachteil der Historie für das Leben' [On the use and abuse of history for life], in *Werke*, I, 253.

20. In the poem 'Enclosure'.

21. Aldous Huxley, *The Perennial Philosophy* (London: Chatto & Windus, 1946), 249–50.

22. Poets in order of quotation: Donne, Emily Brontë, Edward Thomas, Elizabeth Barrett Browning, Keats, Shakespeare, Lawrence.

23. Mimi Khalvati, from a sequence of six ghazals in *The Meanest Flower* (Manchester: Carcanet, 2007).

24. Lawrence, 'Chaos in Poetry', *Selected Literary Criticism*, 90.

25. Hannah Arendt, *Eichmann in Jerusalem* (New York: Penguin Books, 1964), 106.

26. Discussed in Chapter Six of Zygmunt Bauman's *Modernity and the Holocaust* (Oxford: Blackwell, 1989), 151–69.

27. Quoted by Bauman, *Modernity and the Holocaust*, 183.

28. See Auden, *The Dyer's Hand*, 88: 'In our age, the mere making of a work of art is itself a political act. So long as artists exist, making what they please and think they ought to make, even if it is not terribly good, even if it appeals to only a handful of people, they remind the Management of something managers need to be reminded of, that the managed are people with faces, not anonymous numbers...'

4

The Office of Poetry

Human beings are very determinable. Given a role, some official capacity, they incline to behave accordingly. Their *office* shapes them. In 1971 at Stanford University Professor Philip G. Zimbardo conducted an experiment as disturbing as Stanley Milgram's a few years earlier. They advertised for volunteers (who would be paid $15 a day), out of them selected twenty-four healthy, intelligent, middle-class white young college men, divided them arbitrarily into two equal groups: Prisoners and Guards; and sent them home. A few days later nine 'prisoners' were arrested at their homes by the local police force, handcuffed and brought to a jail constructed in the basement of the University, where nine 'guards' had been told to report for duty. The prisoners were stripped, searched, deloused, and clothed in a uniform designed to demean them; each was given a number and addressed only by that. The guards wore mirror sunglasses, making their eyes invisible; they were given no specific instructions, it was left to them to decide what should be done. Scheduled to last two weeks, the experiment was called off after six days. It took only that long for some of the guards to begin behaving sadistically and the others to go along with it; for all solidarity to disintegrate among the prisoners, and for two or three of them to suffer psychological collapse. Very striking also was the obedient and compliant behaviour of the prisoners' parents on visiting day; and a 'parole-board officer' (a former convict) who repeated upon these volunteers the brutalities inflicted on him by just such an officer during his own time in a real jail. Professor Zimbardo himself slid out of his role of experimental psychologist into the role of prison superintendent and by that office found himself increasingly determined.

Guards, prisoners, and indeed most other participants in the Stanford experiment had their humanity reduced by it. Of course, to say that, we must believe human beings to be capable of better than sadism, cowardice, treachery, and compliance. Behind the experiment lingers the old Enlightenment (and un-Christian) belief that Man is born good and social institutions corrupt him. The words 'humane', 'inhuman', 'inhumanity' only mean what they do because we believe or want to believe that humans are naturally good. In German literature and moral philosophy of the eighteenth century 'Mensch' [human being] was the essential category to which appeal could be made through all the world's defacing offices and denominations. Thus in Lessing's *Nathan der Weise* [Nathan the Wise] (ll. 1310–11), Nathan, a Jew, asks of the (at that point) deeply big-oted Christian Templar, 'Sind Christ und Jude eher Christ und Jude, / Als Mensch? [Are Christian and Jew Christian and Jew before they are human beings?']. In Hölderlin's novel *Hyperion* (1797–9), the eponymous hero, a young Greek, after the defeat of all his hopes in his country's failed insurrection against the Turks in 1770, goes into exile in Germany, and finds there nothing for his comfort. He writes of the German people pretty much what Höld-erlin himself thought of them: 'You see working men, but no human beings; thinkers, but no human beings; priests, but no human beings; masters and men, the young and their elders, but no human beings.' That is, he sees people entirely defined by condition or profession, not living in their humanity. He amplifies his criticism:

> To each his own trade, you will say, and I say so too. Only he must follow it with all his soul, not stifle every energy in him that does not quite fit his label, must not in such anxious poverty with such hypocritical literalness be only what he is *called*, with love and all seriousness he should be what he *is*, then the spirit will live in his activity, and if he is boxed into an occupation in which the spirit is not allowed to live, let him thrust it from him in contempt and learn how to plough.
> (III, 153–4)

In *The Good Woman of Sezuan* Brecht asks whether 'ein menschenwür-diges Dasein' [a life worthy of a human being], is possible under the present social order. The phrase itself shows that he, like Marx,

Hölderlin, Lessing, and many others, thought well of humanity and believed human beings deserve better than they presently get.

On the website of the Stanford experiment Professor Zimbardo will take you through it, slide by slide, with a commentary and suggestions for further thought. The guards soon ordered their prisoners to do press-ups, one guard making it harder by treading on the prisoners' backs. That detail is accompanied on the screen with a drawing done by a prisoner in Auschwitz of a guard there treading his boot down on the back of a prisoner doing press-ups. Professor Zimbardo updates the application of his experiment with pictures of American guards abusing Iraqi prisoners in Abu Ghraib. What they demonstrated in Stanford was how biddable people are; which is not necessarily a cause for despair but rather an imperative to set up a social order in which the good in people will be actively fostered; also to be vigilant, and to name and resist all the forces still at loose that demean, corrupt, and abrade our humanity.

Hölderlin's objection is less to the category or office that people inhabit than to how they behave in it, their reduction of themselves in practice to that denomination—everyone head down in his own compartment. But I suppose we can say that some employments will be more likely than others to reduce the humanity of the employees, it would be harder to assert oneself as a whole and humane person in them. The anxiety in Bauman's study (discussed and applied to poetry above) is that the bureaucrat, Eichmann being the extreme example, might so thoroughly define himself by office that there is nothing else to him. He is then, in Marx's term 'entmenscht' [dehumanized, not a human being]. On the other hand, it is quite possible to be less humane—realize oneself less fully, deal less humanely with the people you are bound by office to deal with—than the job permits or encourages: there are bad teachers, bad social workers, bad priests. In Argentina's Dirty War, the torturers would sometimes have doctors in attendance, to assess how much more a victim could take. In 2002, in another dirty war, George Bush's lawyers, John Yoo and Jay Bybee, helpfully interpreted presidential authority and redefined torture so that interrogators might practise it without fear of prosecution.

The question is how fully will the various jobs people do, the offices they hold, the denominations they belong to, allow or encourage them to realize their humanity; and how fully will people realize the humane possibilities in their employment or resist whatever in it would degrade them. And, of course, all employments and categories are themselves more or less diminished or enlarged by the structures and the politics of the state in which they operate. Many people in Britain today do the worthwhile jobs they love not helped but hindered by the institutions employing them. They do the job well, so realizing themselves humanely, almost as an act of opposition to their directed and managed circumstances. To a large extent those dehumanizing circumstances are the product of the ideology of the market. Friedrich Engels observed (in 1844): 'Once a principle has been set in motion it will work itself out, by itself, through all its consequences.'[1] That principle, the market, has in our day spread to most areas of civic life. School exam boards compete for custom, they sell syllabuses and exams. Healthcare and higher education, border control, the transport of prisoners, even their incarceration, are business activities in a market. Within the BBC, a public corporation, there is, needless to say, 'an internal market'. I was at a lecture the other day given by a child-psychotherapist in which he said that he had just begun to hear NHS patients being spoken of as 'material'. In 2011 the management of our census was put out to tender and awarded to Lockheed Martin, an arms dealer. As in the seventeenth century, but with more lethal weaponry and for much better pay, mercenaries fight wars and enforce the aftermath of wars worldwide indifferently for nations with this god or that god on their side. The client relationship and the cash nexus are by now pretty well all-pervasive and by many people taken for granted and accepted as 'just the way world is'. In the service of this ideology—and that's all it is, an ideology, one among many we might choose to shape our lives by, it is not God-given, not inevitable, it is only a thing made up—in the service of this malign fiction structures are put in place, policies made, directives issued, a language used which powerfully determine how people will do their jobs. Many then feel, as I suggested above, that the aspiration to be fully human even in professions chosen as vocations for their intrinsic humanity, must assert itself against a very inimical mindset.

Marx, a radical moralist, described the relationship between capital and labour as one which by its very nature reduces the worker to just such a commodity as those which by his labour he produces. His humanity is replaced by his rising or falling value as a thing to be bought and sold according to the laws of a market obeying nothing but itself. 'The worker sinks to the condition of commodity, of the most miserable commodity...He becomes ever cheaper as commodity the more commodities he produces. The rise in value of the world of things proceeds in direct proportion to the reduction in value of the world of human beings...Production produces the human being not just as commodity, as human commodity, the human being in the function of commodity, it produces him or her, in accordance with that function, as a spiritually and physically dehumanized being' (II, 75, 76, 88). Agreed, in some parts of the world, in some employments, that relationship, though essentially unchanged, has after long struggle been modified and ameliorated in the worker's favour. But the principle is still operative, the relationship—transaction and the cash nexus—is still in place at the centre and often it surfaces into manifestations which are at once entirely consequential and utterly obscene. Daniel Dorling quotes the president of an advertising agency specializing in children: 'Advertising at its best is making people feel that without their product, you're a loser. Kids are very sensitive to that...You open up emotional vulnerabilities, and it's very easy to do [that] with kids because they're the most emotionally vulnerable.' Another spokesperson for the same industry summed it up with even greater candour: 'In our business culture, children are viewed as economic resources to be exploited, just like bauxite or timber.'² The sexualization of children increases their value as consumers, bringing them earlier into the 'adult' market. In the sex *industry* then, it is only to be expected that women and very young girls will be trafficked for prices and in conditions determined by the laws of supply and demand. Civilized nations, signatories to various humane charters, outsource their torture to biddable client states. It is just another transaction, a carrier is needed, a price is agreed, in due course the appropriate department gets invoiced for the hire of the aircraft and the crew's pay and expenses (muffins, bagels, sandwiches, wine, fruit, overnight accommodation), as for the carriage of any cargo. The cargo in question, however, is a human being sedated by rectal suppositories, dressed in a nappy and an orange boiler suit, hooded, muffled and trussed up in the back of the plane.

I turn to poetry for an ally when I worry, as many do, that par-
ticular denominations and categories of social life, be they of race,
creed, class, or employment, reinforce the compliant and uncoura-
geous tendencies in people and so reduce their humanity, lower
their aspirations, impoverish their ability to be with and be respon-
sible for others. Some of that reduction comes from religious beliefs
and their hardening in sects and churches; but more of it, in the
United Kingdom at least, rides on and is enforced by the ever more
pervasive penetration of the principle of the market. Poetry by its
most natural and characteristic workings can help against all funda-
mentalisms and against the conversion of people and their talents
into things to be bought and sold. Poetry is both an activity and a
locus in which we are enabled at least to imagine what autonomy,
self-possession, plurality, and free dealings with others would be like.
The poem in its autonomy, truth embodied in and working through
beauty, says Yes to a life worthy of human beings and No to what-
ever distracts us from desiring or prevents us from attaining it.

What Lawrence claims for the novel—that it can show us life
wholly—I claim for poetry too. He enlists the novel against partial-
ness and absolutism, which in practice amount to the same since to
insist on an absolute is to insist on one thing only, which entails the
denial (or extermination) of all other parts that would interfere with
it. He writes (in 'Why the novel matters'):

> I don't want to grow in any one direction any more. And, if
> I can help it, I don't want to stimulate anybody else into some
> particular direction. A particular direction ends in a *cul-de-sac*.
> We're in a *cul-de-sac* at present....We should ask for no
> absolutes, or absolute. Once and for all and for ever, let us
> have done with the ugly imperialism of any absolute. There is
> no absolute good, there is nothing absolutely right. All things
> flow and change, and even change is not absolute. The whole
> is a strange assembly of apparently incongruous parts, slipping
> past one another...And only in the novel are *all* things given
> full play, or at least, they may be given full play, when we
> realize that life itself, and not inert safety, is the reason for
> living. For out of the full play of all things emerges the only

thing that is anything, the wholeness of a man, the wholeness
of a woman, man alive, and live woman.[3]

Poetry, in my view, can do what the novel can. This is easy to argue
for the great epic poems; their scope and variety are akin to and
indeed were continued in the modern novel. But the typical collec-
tion of forty or so poems, mostly quite short, under a title that may
be the title of one of them, coherent sometimes, perhaps shaped in
sequences, patterned with images, but often only what Hardy (in the
Preface to his *Poems of the Past and the Present*, 1901) calls 'unadjusted
impressions', how does such a volume compete with the novel in
telling life wholly? The total oeuvre of the best poets, even if com-
posed of only such slim volumes, may indeed amount to a whole in
which '*all* things are given full play', the whole of the writer's life,
the whole of his or her felt experience of the world. But really we
don't have to wait for the posthumous Collected Poems. All lyric
poems give glances of the whole of life, and their premise is always
that the life they point to, touch on, glance off, in its entirety exceeds
them—which fact with gladness they demonstrate. And every glance,
every single poem, in its writing and in its being read, has the power
to engage us wholly. 'The poet,' says Coleridge, 'described in ideal
perfection, brings the whole soul of man into activity' (*BL*, 151).
I should say 'the poem' not 'the poet' and with that swap could
leave out 'described in ideal perfection'. That really is what all true
poems do, if we let them. We can be wholly engaged in the appre-
hension of a moment, a glance, of life—knowing it for the living
part of the living whole.

Poetry—literature altogether—offers life wholly. But the human
life being lived in particular time and place is unavoidably partial. All
human living is a struggle to shape a life you can call your own in
the midst of and against many forces determining it for you to your
liking or not. That is obvious and indisputable; and it is little to con-
cede then that many ways of life, many social circumstances, many
employments, many denominations, reduce us into further and fur-
ther partialness. You hope for and, if you have the freedom, you
actively seek an employment which will encourage, not thwart, your
bid to be fully human. Still in whatever you do for a living some
warping of you to fit it will occur—not too much, you might hope,

not too malignant. I heard one of Blair's press secretaries cheerfully admitting on the radio that daily he and his colleagues were obliged to tell lies. It came with the job, it was their *déformation professionelle*. Václav Havel found 'living in truth' easiest as a poet and dramatist, less easy but still possible as an active dissident, but well-nigh impossible (though how he tried!) as Head of State. His life, even more than Brecht's, is exemplary, shiningly figurative. In his first address as President, on New Year's Day 1990, he said: 'Let us teach ourselves that our politics can be not just the art of the possible, especially if that means the art of speculation, calculation, intrigue, secret deals and pragmatic manoeuvring, but that it can even be the art of the impossible, namely the art of improving ourselves and the world.' W. L. Webb, in his obituary of Havel, quotes him as saying: 'Experience of a totalitarian system of the communist type makes emphatically clear one thing which I hope has universal validity: that the prerequisite for everything political is moral. Politics really should be ethics put into practice...This means taking a moral stand not for practical purposes, in the hope that it will bring political results, but as a matter of principle.'[4] Needless to say, in office his views were derided and vehemently opposed by those who wanted instead of communism the wholly unfettered free-for-all capitalist market.

In *The Captive Mind*, Czesław Miłosz describes a person—really, in the fashion of that book, an exemplary figure—whom he calls 'Gamma, the Slave of History'. Gamma aligned himself unambiguously with the Soviet communists when they occupied Poland in 1945 and put his talents as a writer at their disposal. This is Miłosz's verdict on him, fair or not, I don't know, what interests me here is why Miłosz thinks him fit for the office of 'literary politician' and not for that of writer:

> Gamma showed no doubt; his decision was made. I am tempted to explain this on the basis of his voice and his dry, unpleasant laugh, which could lead one to suspect that his emotional life was always rather primitive. He knew anger, hatred, fear, and enthusiasm; but reflective emotion was alien to him – in this lay the weakness of his talent.
>
> Condemned to purely cerebral writing, Gamma clung to doctrine. All he had to say could have been shouted at a meet-

ing or printed in a propaganda leaflet. He could move for-
ward without being swayed by any affective complications; he
was able to express himself in a single tone.[5]

Being able to express yourself 'in a single tone' is a suspect gift; and
being content to would disqualify you from writing poetry. 'Reflec-
tive emotion' and 'affective complications' are the stuff of poetry
and a means to it.

Literature, and the arts altogether, are the chief means by which
human beings attain to consciousness of their condition. Poets and
novelists, makers of fictions, try to say what it is like being human
now; what the truth of our condition is, what responsibilities that
truth entails. Perhaps not many writers have that large project at the
front of their minds as they write; but piece by piece, as they write,
they contribute to the making of human consciousness. And some,
Lawrence very notably, have been well aware of what they are doing.
As the First World War proceeded, he felt certain that the civilized
world's old idea and understanding of itself could not hold. All his
writing, the stuff of it and the very making of sentences, was there-
after a struggle to fashion a consciousness adequate to the fact of the
War, so that people should think, feel, and live differently after and
in accordance with that fact. He wrote:

> It was so foul, and humanity in Europe fell suddenly into such
> ignominy and inhuman ghastliness, that we shall *never* fully
> realize what it was. We just cannot bear it. We haven't the
> soul-strength to contemplate it.
>   And yet, humanity can only finally conquer by realizing. It
> is human destiny, since Man fell into consciousness and self-
> consciousness, that we can only go forward step by step
> through realization, full, bitter, conscious realization.[6]

In *Mrs Dalloway* Virginia Woolf showed a post-war society set on
resuming its old course of life as though nothing had changed. But
one character, Septimus, can't resume. In him the fact of the War
is unliveable with. Lawrence died in1930; Woolf killed herself in
1941. Much has 'happened' since then.[7]

Making a consciousness fit for now must involve realizing what
the race we are members of has done. Long before the First World

War had even begun to be truthfully taken in, came Auschwitz, Hiroshima, the Gulags, Pol Pot...Humans have a lot of catching up to do. Living in truth in the here and now would mean living in a consciousness comprehending our past. Would that in practice be desirable or even possible? Septimus impales himself on the railings. Robert Graves wrote *Goodbye to All That*, to be rid of the War; and he set up his own poetic myth—the White Goddess—as a new order against the order of the old world that commanded poison gas. Still, in the last years of his life, when the power of speech had deserted him, he sat staring in blank terror—at what? Primo Levi, in poetry and prose, exactly and fully wrote about the death camps: but could not live in the consciousness that by his witness he helped make. Consciousness may inhibit action, may impair life itself. Conscience doth make cowards of us all. So what is the point of enlisting poetry and fiction in an aspiration to live in truth, in a consciousness adequate to what we have done and might do? The simple answer is that most people most of the time live in a state much closer to total *un*consciousness than to any degree of consciousness even half-ways adequate to our real situation. We don't yet need to worry about living in total consciousness but we do need to worry about living in near-*un*consciousness. Living in ignorance means living partially. We don't yet need to worry about the consequences of living wholly but we are confronted every day by the consequences of living *very* partially. Some leaders get to power by a frightening reduction and narrowing of their humanity—and reduce it and narrow it further in office; and take decisions in the blinkered encasement of their narrowness that profoundly and often catastrophically affect the brief lives of millions of people. We do need to worry about that.

The poet holds and practises the office of poetry but is, of course, in his or her proper person, less than it. So in speaking of the office of poetry I hold no brief for how the individual poet lives his or her own life. Coleridge (*BL*, 235), said of Wordsworth, 'Such as he *is*: so he *writes*'; and I could name a few poets for whom, in the good sense Coleridge intended, that would be true. But really the claim for consonance begs too many questions to be of much use here. For one thing, all poets, however large and universal their achievement, live as they manage to live in the real circumstances of particular time and place; which is to say they perforce live partially. Add to that, the obvious fact that they are as liable as anyone else to muddle, prejudice, envy, self-interest, small-mindedness, mania, depression, and failure of the will to live. There will be a difference between the poet—'the bundle of accident and incoherence that sits down to breakfast'[8]—and the poem, and it will be a difference of less and more fully realized humanity. Consider the lines:

> No longer mourn for me when I am dead
> Then you shall hear the surly sullen bell
> Give warning to the world that I am fled
> From this vile world, with vilest worms to dwell:
> Nay, if you read this line, remember not
> The hand that writ it, for I love you so
> That I in your sweet thoughts would be forgot,
> If thinking on me then should make you woe.

We can't know, and it doesn't matter, whether Shakespeare himself was capable in his real life of the unselfishness the poem expresses. All we know for certain is that he was capable of imagining it—such unselfishness that the speaker in the poem would rather be forgotten than give pain to the beloved by being remembered—and could word it so well that we reading the lines more than four hundred years later can imagine such unselfishness too. The poet will often, perhaps always, be less than the poem. This is clearer—it is soon made known—in our age of published diaries, collected letters, and exhaustive personal biographies. The Larkin who in his letters can be foul-mouthed and misogynistic is the same man who wrote 'Wedding-Wind', in the young wife's voice:

> ...Now in the day
> All's ravelled under the sun by the wind's blowing.
> He has gone to look at the floods, and I
> Carry a chipped pail to the chicken-run,
> Set it down, and stare. All is the wind
> Hunting through clouds and forests, thrashing
> My apron and the hanging cloths on the line.
> Can it be borne, this bodying-forth by wind
> Of joy my actions turn on, like a thread
> Carrying beads? Shall I be let to sleep

Now this perpetual morning shares my bed?
Can even death dry up
These new delighted lakes, conclude
Our kneeling as cattle by all-generous waters?

All-generous. The woman's joy is lifted further by the wind, expressed
and heightened by the objects she contemplates. But 'we receive but
what we give'. She participates in the world outside, out of her centre
she extends her joy into the life around, shares herself, shares in it.

Poetry offers to our imagination and to our feelings a greater
humanity than most of us, and even its writers, are capable of in
everyday life. Some will, some won't, need persuading that this
experience, engendered by art, matters; and certainly it is quite hard
to define how and why it matters even if we are sure it does. Miłosz
observes, 'Never has there been a close study of how necessary to a
man are the experiences which we clumsily call aesthetic.'[9]

I want now to look at some writing which is not poetry and is not
seeking to give the reader such an experience. Poetry being made of
words and those words being open to all to use as they please, I
might distinguish the language of poetry, in comparison with other
kinds of language, by calling it *unrestricted*. Most other discourse—
writing or speaking—is determined, which in practice means
restricted, by function, the requirements of a particular occasion, or
by office.

It may seem odd to call the language of poetry unrestricted. The
German phrase 'gebundene Rede' [bound speech] means verse; and
throughout most of its history verse has indeed been bound—into
metre, rhyme, alliterative patterns, stanzas, genres, and its tones of
voice and its vocabulary have been restricted and distinguished from
those of common speech. Now in much European and North Amer-
ican poetry many or even most of those restrictions don't apply.
Certainly, whether you bind your poetic language in rhythm and
metre or not, it and its tones may be as comprehensively various as
you please. So in that sense at least modern poetry has a freedom
which for Sappho, Christine de Pisan, and Christina Rossetti it did
not have. But that expansion or liberation does not mean that for
the last hundred years poetry has been getting steadily more expres-
sive. However tightly disciplined, poetry always has been what now,

less disciplined, it still is: the medium in which the most can be said best. The freedom of poetry to do what it is meant to do never was reduced by the various conventions under which it operated and is not increased now by the loosening or loss of such conventions. Form doesn't hinder, it enables, extends, and intensifies. Poets writing now know that as well as their predecessors did, and so adopt or devise such formal disciplines as will help them in their freedom to say whatever they wish to say as tellingly as possible. The essential freedom and unrestrictedness of poetry is not a function of form but lies in every poem's ability (and responsibility) to quicken us to the condition of being human.

Two passages of prose

Into a heavy 10 inch frying pan or sauté pan put enough olive oil to cover the surface. Let the oil warm over low heat then put in the onions. They should stew gently, without frying, for about 7 minutes. Add the crushed garlic cloves, then the fresh tomatoes. With the pan uncovered, increase the heat, so that the water content of the tomatoes evaporates rapidly. Add seasonings of salt and a very little sugar. When the fresh tomatoes have reduced almost to a pulp add the tinned ones if you are using them. There is no need to chop them. Simply spoon them into the pan with some of their juice and crush them with a wooden spoon.[10]

The canals of England are mainly the creation of the last forty years of the eighteenth century and the first quarter of the nineteenth, and they introduced a number of distinctive changes into the landscape. Not only did they bring stretches of water into country often lacking in them, as in many parts of the Midlands, with consequent changes in bird and plant life, but they also brought – mostly for the first time – aqueducts, cuttings and embankments, tunnels, locks, lifts and inclined planes, and many attractive bridges, and they greatly influenced the growth and appearance of many towns. One town, indeed, was entirely the creation of canals (Stourport in Worcestershire) and is worth seeing solely on that account.[11]

A chief characteristic of such language is that it has an agreed pur-
pose, to do and convey some definite thing. The language *serves that
purpose*, it subordinates itself to the purpose. Nowhere does it become
an end in itself, it does not draw attention to itself. The more it
induced us to attend to it in itself, the less well it would serve its
purpose. This is a question of genre, of what is proper to the job in
hand. I admit, the categories are not watertight; but most often it
would be merely distracting and would undermine the purpose if,
say, a piece of prose explaining the workings of the Large Hadron
Collider suddenly fell into a dactyllic metre or allowed words in
proximity to rhyme. Functional language can give pleasure, of
course: the pleasure that comes from fitness for the purpose, econ-
omy, clarity. So if I say that in comparison with the language of
poetry such language is restricted language I mean that approvingly
not critically. It is doing what is asked of it.

Reading a book or an essay *about* poetry, if the writer, for the
argument, quotes a poem, it is very easy to feel by the different
kinds of attention the discursive prose and the poem embedded in it
require, just how differently those two languages work. Often indeed
the juxtaposition, giving each its proper due, will be unmanageable.
Most likely the poem, demanding more, will get less, and will be
subordinated, as material, to the argument; an abuse only justifiable
if the prose helps us back to the poem later, for a better reading.

Keats said that 'poetry should surprise by a fine excess' (*Letters*,
p. 69); the 'excess' being, perhaps, everything in poetic language
which exceeds what a sentence would need most simply to convey
its burden of fact, information, or opinion. You can see such excess
in Shakespeare, in speeches whose essential function is to relate an
event or convey some factual information. For example, in *Antony
and Cleopatra* (1.4.48–56), the Second Messenger, arriving to tell
Octavius that Pompey and the pirates Menas and Menacrates have
become bolder, says it in these words:

> Caesar, I bring thee word
> Menacrates and Menas, famous pirates,
> Makes the sea serve them, which they ear and wound
> With keels of every kind. Many hot inroads
> They make in Italy – the borders maritime
> Lack blood to think on't – and flush youth revolt.

No vessel can peep forth but 'tis as soon
Taken as seen; for Pompey's name strikes more
Than could his war resisted.

This passage, nearly every line of which is glossed in the Arden Shakespeare, abundantly exceeds what would be necessary to put Octavius in possession of the facts; it exceeds its basic function, which is to report.

Two poems

I could have chosen poems doing things more obviously suitable only to poetry; but these two demonstrate how differently poetry and prose work because both have an *ostensible* purpose—the first description, the second narration—which prose could serve just as well or better.

John Clare: Emmonsails Heath in Winter

I love to see the old heaths withered brake
Mingle its crimpled leaves with furze & ling
While the old Heron from the lonely lake
Starts slow & flaps his melancholly wing
& oddling crow in idle motions swing
On the half rotten ash trees topmost twig
Beside whose trunk the gipsey makes his bed
Up flies the bouncing woodcock from the brig
Where a black quagmire quakes beneath the tread
The fieldfare chatters in the whistling thorn
& for the awe round fields and closen rove
& coy bumbarrels twenty in a drove
Flit down the hedgrows in the frozen plain
& hang on little twigs & start again

Clare's first book (1820) was called *Poems Descriptive of Rural Life and Scenery*. He came in at the end of a public liking for such poetry started by James Thomson (*The Seasons*, 1726–30) whom he greatly admired. 'Emmonsails Heath in Winter' is taken from *The Midsummer Cushion*, Clare's fourth book (1832), for which he could not find a publisher. Clare wrote scores of sonnets and in most of them—here, for example—seems bent on proving that the form cannot possibly contain all he has to say. Several times in *The Midsummer*

Cushion, under the same title, he runs on out of one sonnet into two or three. 'A Walk' and 'Footpaths', appropriately, each take him through five. The sonnet with its rhyme scheme (here, and often, not *very* strict) serves him to dip into the flow of life, show some glimpses of it, let them go. Really, his brief in all his 'descriptive' poems, whether they begin with the words or not, is to show the things he loves to see, to show why, to make the love felt. He reciprocrates, he *loves back*, by saying exactly and adequately what they are like, how they live and have their being.

Description, in prose or poetry, is a difficult business because the writer has to arrange in words in sequence the details that in reality co-exist. Reading, if you wanted to see in the mind what the writer was describing, you would have to assemble all the parts in their spatial relations, which is laborious and, at any length, impossible. The eye at the scene itself does it easily, instantaneously. But no such labour is necessary reading 'descriptive' poetry if it really is poetry, because the intention is not, in any important degree, to describe. Clare follows the natural bent of language and moves from detail to detail, rhyme to rhyme, in a list, as though it didn't matter where he starts, finishes, or what he puts in or leaves out. And yet it does. He signals an infinity he can't and wouldn't wish to contain—and marshals a few glimpses into a shape in which, since this is a poem not a piece of descriptive prose, they belong, they exceed themselves in their reach and connectedness. Within the—so to speak—*temporary* container of the sonnet, they sort intriguingly and touchingly with one another: the heron, the crow, the woodcock, the fieldfare, the drove of 'bumbarrels' (long-tailed tits) make a sequence out of solitariness into company. The fieldfare, usually seen in flocks, first have the singular 'chatters', then the plural 'rove'. The thorn, which stands alone without a rhyme, is more likely a hedge, as in the following line, than a single tree. But the solitary observer views his alter ego in the gipsy under the half rotten ash on which is perched the oddling crow. Much love is here; but also loneliness, isolation, decay, the uncanny. There's a safe bridge, but under it a quagmire which if you tread there—and how would you know this if you hadn't?—quakes. But the woodcock bounces up, the fieldfare and the tits go after food, they answer back against the killing cold—chatter against the wind's whistling, flitting in company against a killing loneliness. These are minute particulars at their holiest. And the language of them does indeed draw attention to itself—'crimpled', 'oddling', 'awe', 'closen', 'coy'—and can bear it, it gives delight, it flashes in all directions, retarding the onward march of the rhyming lines, multiplying the possibilities of our reading. Clare's own dialect words, his waverings of singular and plural between noun and verb, quicken our attention, we are alerted, we begin to see. Unpunctuated, no full stop, as the poem ends, the bumbarrels start again. This man on the brink of half a lifetime of alienation watches them go and blesses them with rhymes.

Richard Wilbur: April 5, 1974

> The air was soft, the ground still cold.
> In the dull pasture where I strolled
> Was something I could not believe.
> Dead grass appeared to slide and heave,
> Though still too frozen-flat to stir,
> And rocks to twitch, and all to blur.
> What was this rippling of the land?
> Was matter getting out of hand
> And making free with natural law?
> I stopped and blinked, and then I saw
> A fact as eerie as a dream.
> There was a subtle flood of steam
> Moving upon the face of things.
> It came from standing pools and springs
> And what of snow was still around;
> It came of winter's giving ground
> So that the freeze was coming out,
> As when a set mind, blessed by doubt,
> Relaxes into mother-wit.
> Flowers, I said, will come of it.

This is a narrative poem in so far as it tells of a walk during which a phenomenon was observed that at first puzzled then became intelligible to the narrator. So the process of the poem, on the surface at least, is from puzzlement to understanding. For a few lines of prose that would suffice. But the ten rhyming couplets, four iambic beats to a line, are a signal that more is being offered. All the rhymes are full and monosyllabic; but, though so definite in themselves, they do not serve to chop the poem up into ten separate units. On the contrary, no rhyming couplet is a finished unit of sense. The sense always reaches over the rhyming word and is completed in the new rhyme's first line. This principle of fluidity against fixity is a major constituent of the poem's total sense. Also, the rhythm (how we actually say the lines) plays agreeably over and against the demands of the metre: in no line do speech and metrical requirement coincide too heavily. Something natural—how we speak—flows through the formal structure. The verse is not allowed to *set*. And that—a matter of poetic devising—is, in essence, the whole poem. The surface or ostensible progress of the poem is very simple: the strange phenomenon, the solid earth appearing to stir, ripple, and flow, line by line being enacted in the movement of the verse as I described it above, soon receives its explanation in the words 'the freeze was coming out'. And there the ostensible narrative purpose—puzzlement, explanation—is fulfilled. But it can't halt there: we want a rhyme for 'out'; and get it in the first half of a likeness 'As when a set mind, blessed by doubt...'; which might be thought the clinching part (by means of a simile) of the explanation for the whole mystery so far; but instead it applies that mystery's being explained to a human movement quite beyond it. 'Relaxes into mother wit', the explanatory application of the whole phenomenon, is an unrhyming couplet. We want one more line, to conclude the poem with a rhyme. And it is: 'Flowers, I said, will come of it'—which harks back as literal truth to the melting of the ground but is now (after the previous two lines) afforced with the figurative sense that these are the benefits of a set mind's being blessed by doubt and relaxing into mother-wit. The line 'Moving upon the face of things', alluding to Genesis 1:2: 'And the Spirit of God moved upon the face of the waters', suggests that we might be, like the earth, abundantly creative if we let our minds be unsettled whenever they harden into certainties. The title is a date: on that day something important was realized. Reading, and realizing, we could add a date of our own.

Edward Thomas criticized William Gibson for 'writing about things instead of creating them'.[12] Clare and Wilbur, in those examples above, exceed the ostensible genre (descriptive, narrative), and do not merely *write about* the subject. They make something of it, they create something. And that something is a poem.

Saying the human

In any social context in which the citizens' humanity is reduced and confined, in which their aspiration to realize themselves fully is hampered or stifled, poetry helps because, by its very nature, by virtue of office, it continually and thoroughly *says the human*. 'Poetry,' says Shelley, 'is the record of the best and happiest moments of the happiest and best minds';[13] but in fact poetry is much more than that. There are of course in the whole corpus of poetry innumerable glimpses and indeed some very ample images of human beings at their morally best—Chaucer's poor clerk, Goldsmith's schoolmaster, Wordsworth's Beaupuy; and moments of happiness abound; still, all that is only a part of poetry's total brief and achievement, which is to demonstrate entirely what being human is like, how human beings have lived, live now, might live. And included in that 'entirely' are poems such as Donne's 'The Apparition' which are inspired not by the unselfishness of Shakespeare's Sonnet 71 but by a vengeful possessiveness towards the beloved. All that is and must be there in poetry, the unselfish, the noble, the murderous, the petty, the loving kindness, the spite, the hatred, the ordinary decency, the passionate demands. By saying the human in its superabundant variety, in itself and in its dealings with the 'whole circumambient universe',[14] poems hold up a measure that any state's politics can be measured by, a demand by which that politics may be held to account. Poems say, This is what the citizens are like, in their common humanity and in their myriad kinds of uniqueness, they are not there to fit the state, the state is there to fit them, serve them, aid them in their aspiration to the free development of their social and individual selves. So under any politics, under any social order, by which the citizens are not given that aid and encouragement but are instead stunted and thwarted in their legitimate demands for a freely self-made identity, turned to things in a market to be bought and sold, reduced, corrupted, demeaned into the lowest versions of being human, under any such ideology and its practice by government, poetry is a very present help and ally in the necessary revolt.

The extremest form of reduction and denial of the citizens' humanity is practised by totalitarian states such as Nazi Germany. *Gleichschaltung* [co-ordination] is a term taken from electrical engineering where it means the synchronizing or making compatible of different currents, so that the whole works smoothly. *Der gleichgestaltete Staat* is a state co-ordinated in that mechanical fashion. You can see what it *looks like*—the drilled people—in Leni Riefenstahl's film *Triumph des Willens* (1935) [triumph of the will]. The motivation in the making of such a state is a pathological purism. Every human element that does not naturally fit or cannot be made to fit into its workings will be expelled (into exile) or exterminated (in the camps). All purisms and fundamentalisms are pathologically *partial*. They can employ only a very small part of a citizen's (or devotee's) humanity and must block, eject, or eradicate the rest. Totalitarian states are notably humourless and cannot tolerate irony because in irony lives the possibility of at least two points of view.

Reduced to the working bits of a machine, humans lose their individualities, their voices, their faces. I have already praised poetry for its love and celebration of particularities. All its figurative reach is got from an exact and loving knowledge of particular human beings in their dealings with the world in particular time and place. In the mechanically co-ordinated state and in its machinery of extermination (the bureaucracy, the railway lines, the timetables, the gas chambers, the crematoria) those distinguishing features are obliterated. Public memorials, naming all the names, are one way of insisting that the murdered were individual people. Modern warfare too, killing in millions, requires its monuments, like that at Thiepval for the Somme's more than 70,000 unburied dead, all the names, among them my grandfather, 8571 Private J. W. Gleave of Number 2 Platoon, 'A' Company, the 17th Manchester Regiment, and before that of 57 Liverpool Street, Salford 5. For my poem about him, or about my grandmother, Bertha Gleave, living in the loss of him, I took as epigraph four words from Part 7 of David Jones's *In Parenthesis*: 'So many without memento'.[15] Poetry, born among particular people, helps in the remembering, which is to say in the continuing love, of them, when they are blown to bits and strewn around some foreign field. And the same onus, to remember, to name, rests on poetry now and still. Who is that trussed and hooded cargo? What is his name? Who misses him?

Havel understood his Czechoslovakia, 'a post-totalitarian society' is his term for it, to be a fabricated thing entirely opposed to what he called simply (and to my mind adequately) 'the aims of life'. Dissidence, for him and his comrades in Charter 77, was the answering back of the aims of life against the state which denied them; and writing and the other arts were a chief agent of that answering back. We don't live in a post-totalitarian society in Britain, we live in a democracy but one which risks becoming what Havel in the 1970s saw already breeding in his country, a society not furthering but deflecting and diverting the citizen's energies away from an authentic life into 'what is really a desperate substitute for living'. He asks:

> What has happened to the idea that a man should live in full enjoyment of social and legal justice, have a creative share in economic and political power, be raised on high in his human dignity and become truly himself? Instead of free economic decision-sharing, free participation in political life and free intellectual advancement, all he is actually offered is a chance freely to choose which washing machine or refrigerator he wants to buy.[16]

For us too, our democracy notwithstanding, the aims of life have been pretty effectively buried under the more easily and for some very profitably achievable aims of the market. Shopping in lieu of living; the whole duty of man reduced to consuming and the rights of man and the citizen reduced to choice among unnecessary commodities. This means that many if not most people nowadays in the UK if asked to define the aims of life would do so in the terms not of being but of having. Poetry can help radicalize and refine that definition, shift it more towards the terms of being, and so help an electorate become more finely demanding. Politicians themselves— even the good men and women among them who entered politics to help—are unlikely to wish to radicalize their electorate's demands. Office narrows their own definitions of the human. No politician lately—so far as I know—has asked the citizens do they not feel ashamed to be addressed and appealed to the way they are. There is great cause for such shame which, admitted and tapped into, might contribute powerfully to the total energy of revolt. An electorate quickened by the shamefulness of what is offered them, quickened into a better opinion of themselves, would not vote for candidates still offering them more of the old and demeaning stuff.

But—a big but—as things get materially worse for more and more people (though never for the ones telling us we are all in this together) the aims of life will very understandably be narrowed and reduced to one: staying alive. So of course there has to be a politics that serves, in strict priority, the needs of the needy first. There was such a politics once, in aspiration and even in practice too: from each according to his means, to each according to his needs. That itself, radically espoused and practised, would make the start on the way of the aims of life. Poetry and fiction must keep saying the human, giving the measure, insisting on what individual human beings are actually like, and in so doing quickening and radicalizing the demands for a society in which, in Havel's phrase, it would be possible to live 'within the truth'.[17]

The arts in our democracy are the Extra-Parliamentary Opposition. Unlike the Official (Her Majesty's Loyal) Opposition, they are not seeking office and so will not trim the truth to that compelling interest. It is not their job to formulate alternative policies, which in the present impasse are for the most part only slight variations on the old and ineffectual tune. The responsibility of the EPO consists in continually saying the human and in being a locus of freedom in which the imagination can have its way. Much political thinking is merely reactive—to the 'other' party or, even more worryingly, to crises caused by mechanisms beyond control. Even the good and intelligent in power look powerless, unfree. They are dictated to by office and by events. They react as best they can, unfreely, hampered, even helpless. The arts, by virtue of office, have freedom and, having it, are a main (though not the only) source and safeguard of the utopian thinking without which, as is obvious, we will never mend our living and might not even survive. It matters, how we think. We know that mindsets can be changed—in laws and attitudes concerning, for example, race relations and sexuality there have been changes almost unimaginable before the Second World War. Now even bigger shifts of thinking are necessary. They will only come from the politicians if the electorate itself demands them. The arts are qualified to encourage those demands, and among the arts literature pre-eminently, by the free play of the imagination, in words.

Utopia, by its etymology, is a not-place, it is no place, nowhere; which gives it the freedom to be anywhere. Locate it where you will, whole or in fragments. The very idea of Utopia serves the principle of hope. Poetry is charged with that hope, every poem is a hopeful particle. The utopian charge is close to what Nietzsche meant by *Wahn* [illusion], a freely conceived image or imagery whose value is to be assessed by what it does, how productive it is, not by how faithfully it reiterates the present facts. He likens it to the atmosphere without which a planet cannot live.[18] As the power of imagination, the engine of productive images, fails, so life on the planet dies. I know this mythopoeic gift at its largest in the poetry of Hölderlin. Born, like Wordsworth, Beethoven, and Hegel, in 1770, he was of the generation that hoped, for a while at least, that, as the century turned, the ideals of the American and the French Revolutions would be realized on earth. In essence this is an earthly version of the millennial thinking of some strains of Christianity; and for Hölderlin the New Republic was to be a state in which, here on earth, a life 'voll göttlichen Sinns' [full of a sense of the divine] would be made possible. His poetic thinking has a fluid tripartite structure: he looks back to Periclean Athens as the locus of such a republic and forward to some fitting new form of it, soon; but lives meanwhile in a modernity offensive and distressing to anyone with such hopes. His gets his vision by remembering and imagining an ideal past (the Greek polis) and projects it into an imminent future, for realization on the real earth. Love and friendship, and the beauties of Nature in his native Swabia and in Greece, act as guarantors of the possibility of the better future. He loved Susette Gontard, the wife of a Frankfurt banker whose personal motto was 'les affaires avant tout' [business before all else], and addresses and celebrates her in his poems as the Athenian woman or Diotima. Because of her, and in despite of the bankers, he called Frankfurt what Pindar had called Delphi: 'the navel of the earth'. In poem after poem, odes, elegies, hymns in Classical style, he built at a cosmos whose poles were Greece and Hesperia and, at the heart of Hesperia, his homeland in which, like Athens after Marathon, the New Republic would arise.

All longing back risks deteriorating into useless nostalgia; the longing forward, as it seeks fulfilment in the social and political, ends again and again in bitter disappointment. But this dynamism is itself utopian: proof that the desire for a better state and belief in its possibility have not been eradicated. Romantics understood it as an inborn need in human beings to find in the world outside them counterparts and realizations—what Goethe called 'antwortende Gegenbilder' [answering images and correlatives][19]—of their most heartfelt desires and aspirations. Such, in Shelley's view, is the driving force of love: to want living antitypes, to seek after them: 'So soon as this want or power is dead, man becomes the living sepulchre of himself, and what yet survives is the mere husk of what once he was.'[20] 'Want or power' says it exactly. Out of the felt lack springs the desire and the force to make it good.

A prime mover in the bid for a present and future happiness is memory: the memory that there once was, or, at the very least, there was once the possibility of, happiness. Just outside the town of Murat in the Auvergne, on the edge of the high sheer stump of an extinct volcano, there is a rusty iron noticeboard on which is written this line from a poem by Prévert: 'Si tu crois que le bonheur t'oublie, ne l'oublie jamais tout à fait' [If you believe happiness is forgetting you, don't you ever quite forget it (or better, for the feeling of the verse: her or him)]. Much of the life-asserting dynamism of poetry is active in that one line. Happiness itself needs to be remembered, which is to say believed in. Forget it, in unhappiness, and you have nothing to strive to recover and outbid. Prévert's line makes you feel that happiness herself, happiness himself, will drift away disconsolate and unhappy if not sufficiently believed in, loved, and cherished. And you may be wrong in thinking yourself forgotten. Then, forgetting, you would be responsible for the loss. The line makes you an agent in the making of your own life. There it is: a line of poetry on a rusty board at a place where you might extinguish every possibility. Perhaps on the edge of that precipice above Murat poetry has proved its virtue by making something *not* happen.

Everyone leaves childhood and, if it was a happy time, may hark back to it—remember and imagine it—as a force for good in adult life. Clare's childhood and in it his love for Mary Joyce were lost to

him beyond the fences of Enclosure. He is the very figure of expro-
priation. Still in him, in his poems, the want *and* power lives and
breathes, sometimes as elegy, sometimes as present idyll in those
repeated opening lines: 'I love…I love to see…' But what if there
never was a childhood fit to be looked at? What if there is nothing
to go back to that might help? In the eyes of someone I was encour-
aging to write, I once saw my Romanticism viewed incredulously:

Teacher

This child's verdict on
Herself is final. I have
No good in me and hopes of any
None. The cuts
Have reached her throat. Go back
I said, before the fall and grasp
Any scrap of innocence
For a proof and clue. With that
We might begin again. Her look!
Something like pity
As though against her heart
She must enlighten me about the Tooth Fairy
And the apparent blue of heaven.
With that
Something like pity in her look
I tried again.

Novalis said of Paradise that it was 'so to speak, *strewn* all over the
earth and for that reason become so unrecognizable'. Like Orpheus?
And now 'its scattered features are to be reunited—its skeleton to be
filled out'. We are charged with 'the regeneration of Paradise'.[21]
Meanwhile there is a bright litter of Paradise over this earth. Our
modern version of the myth might be rather that, without hope of
any total recovery or regeneration, we may, with luck, continually
come across odd bits, enough and often enough, to keep the idea of
it alive in us: stray epiphanies, reminders, promptings, goadings,
moments of idyll in personal localities, local loyalties, local friend-
ship and love. As here, commemorated forever in Edward Thomas's
poem on the subject of his walking and talking with Robert Frost:

The sun used to shine while we two walked
Slowly together, paused and started

Again, and sometimes mused, sometimes talked
As either pleased, and cheerfully parted

Each night. We never disagreed
Which gate to rest on. The to be
And the late past we gave small heed.
We turned from men or poetry

To rumours of the war remote
Only till both stood disinclined
For aught but the yellow flavorous coat
Of an apple wasps had undermined;

Or a sentry of dark betonies,
The stateliest of small flowers on earth,
At the forest verge; or crocuses
Pale purple as if they had their birth

In sunless Hades fields. The war
Came back to mind with the moonrise
Which soldiers in the east afar
Beheld then. Nevertheless, our eyes

Could as well imagine the Crusades
Or Caesar's battle. Everything
To faintness like those rumours fades –
Like the brook's water glittering

Under the moonlight – like those walks
Now – like us two that took them, and
The fallen apples, all the talks
And silences – like memory's sand

When the tide covers it late or soon,
And other men through other flowers
In those fields under the same moon
Go talking and have easy hours.

In August 1914 Thomas and his family were on holiday at Leading-
ton, on the Gloucestershire/Herefordshire border, Robert Frost and
his family were at Little Iddens, nearby. A year later, having enlisted,
and recalling their walks, Thomas wrote to Frost: 'Ledington...seems
purely paradisal, with Beauty of Bath apples Hesperidean lying with
thunder dew on the warm ground.'[22] Pausing and concentrating

entirely on 'the yellow flavorous coat / Of an apple wasps had undermined', the two poets were doing as Blake said we should: attending to 'minute particulars'. That act of attention and the words of it are themselves 'paradisal', they in the whole poem are abiding proof long after the poet's death of how well a human being can live. Edward Thomas was killed at Arras on 9 April 1917. Almost twenty years later Frost wrote 'Iris by Night', recalling in grateful wonderment another of their walks, coming down off the Malverns at nightfall in a mist, and a small rainbow forming which

> ...lifted from its dewy pediment
> Its two mote-swimming many-colored ends
> And gathered them together in a ring.
> And we stood in it softly circled round
> From all division time or foe can bring
> In a relation of elected friends.

We can fairly say of 'Iris by Night', as of 'The sun used to shine while we two walked...': this lasts, it reaches out from the two friends, now both 'in sunless Hades', in words into the lives of anyone who will listen.

Frost prefaces the forming of the encircling rainbow with these lines: 'And then we were vouchsafed the miracle / That never yet to other two befell...' And perhaps Iris never has distinguished two friends in quite that way before or since. But it is not only remarkable events that are unique. No human experience, however banal, can exactly repeat itself. That is why poetry, responsible for the particular, must come at similar experiences again and again. People rightly feel moment by moment their being in the world to be unique. In the rush of extraordinary poems written by Thomas Hardy after the death of his first wife, Emma, is one, 'At Castle Boterel', which discloses the pathos inherent in the fact of the uniqueness of all human experience. Hardy, going back forty years to the places of his courtship, sees in the poem the two of them climbing the steep road out of Boscastle, having alighted 'to ease the sturdy pony's load / When he sighed and slowed'. Then come the poem's central three stanzas, the heart of the grief:

> What we did as we climbed, and what we talked of
> Matters not much, nor to what it led, –

> Something that life will not be balked of
> > Without rude reason till hope is dead,
> > > And feeling fled.

> It filled but a minute. But was there ever
> > A time of such quality, since or before,
> In that hill's story? To one mind never,
> > > Though it has been climbed, foot-swift, foot-sore
> > > > By thousands more.

> Primaeval rocks form the road's steep border,
> > And much have they faced there, first and last,
> Of the transitory in Earth's long order;
> > > But what they record in colour and cast
> > > > Is – that we two passed.

Unique it is, but thousands of readers rightly and properly have appropriated the experience into their own lives. Perhaps they walked up that road in the dark, or some similar road, or never did anything of the sort. If the poem works in them they acknowledge the human, they acknowledge it theirs, the first love, Beeny Cliff, the 'opal and the sapphire of that wandering western sea', then the long failure and alienation and the resurgence of love in a terrible grief, unique and common, felt as common, able to be made one's own, able to be shared, because bodied forth in a poem as unique. Those two passed—they walked up that road on a particular evening in March 1870. One died in 1912, the other in 1928. Edward Thomas died in 1917, Robert Frost in 1963—passed. And the living translate the poems into further and further life.

In the summer of 1914 Rilke was one of a few people sent a specially printed pre-publication copy of Volume 4 of the new edition of Hölderlin's works. The editor, Norbert von Hellingrath, was killed two years later at Verdun, aged twenty-eight. That fourth volume contains much of Hölderlin's late poetry, the very heart of his achievement, unknown till then. On a blank page at the back, Rilke wrote a poem addressed to him, knowing him for a predecessor, because for Hölderlin too the premise of the poems was the manifest absence of the conditions for a life 'worthy of human beings'. In 1908 Rilke had written an elegy for Wolf Graf von Kalkreuth, a young poet who had killed himself, lamenting in him the failure of the will not to despair (failure of the will *to write*). The poem concludes: 'Wer spricht von Siegen? Überstehn ist alles.' [Who speaks of winning? Survival is all.] The very premise of Rilke's *Duino Elegies*, in their composition straddling the war, is a thorough disillusionment, the post-Nietzsche *table rase*. The *Elegies* are driven by the will to make sense, to uphold to the angels human lives and deeds fit to be looked at, to assert our value in the teeth of so much flatly denying it. That is a utopianism for our times: the nearly desperate bid to make sense, not to go under in the welter of violent non-sense. Aragon, Neruda, Brecht, Darwish, great lyric poets and *poètes engagés*, show again and again, and by showing assert, the value of the life still being lived under siege, in the midst of brutalities, under the threat of ideologies so vile they would stop the very breath of any hope. The poems insist: there is better than this, we are fit for better than this. As soon as we stop believing and saying that then indeed we are the sepulchre and dead and buried in it. But poetry is tough, it lives. Brecht owned a little wooden image of the Chinese god of happiness, mass produced, cheaply available, the god who, however maltreated, tormented, defaced, and dismembered, was finally unkillable. He dances on the gallows. Brecht commented: the human demand for happiness cannot be exterminated.[23]

For poetry to carry the utopian charge it is not necessary, indeed now it would seem almost improper, to offer any vision as large and coherent as Hölderlin's (which, of course, does not lessen our need for his vision in our times). The charge is there whether such fully realized humanity is imagined and presented in the poem or not. It is there even in the depiction of the opposite—alienation, loss, barbarity (Hölderlin does that too). By its very act, even in saying the worst, by its rhythms, by its beauty, by its tough and agile vitality, poetry asserts the hope of better. For there is no such thing as a nihilistic poem. Poets are makers: in the form of a poem, in beauty, they make sense.

Lear, evicted from the office of kingship, suffers a violent extension of sympathy into other lives. Before he will go into the hovel Kent has found for him—in which Poor Tom is accommodated—he kneels and prays:

> Poor naked wretches, wheresoe'er you are,
> That bide the pelting of this pitiless storm
> How shall your houseless heads and unfed sides,

> Your looped and windowed raggedness, defend you,
> From seasons such as these? O, I have ta'en
> Too little care of this.

$$(3.4.28-33)$$

That quickening of sympathy is precisely what poetry is good for. We all take 'too little care', don't notice enough, don't attend closely enough, sympathize, act in sympathy enough. One very encouraging fact about poetry now, over the past few decades getting ever stronger, is its widening of sympathy, from more perspectives. Poetry has never been more various in its voices, its speakers, its *dramatis personae*, and so in its appeal. In Britain now we have a poetry beginning to be truly representative of the national mix—the classes, the races, the regions, the vernaculars, the conflicting interests; which greatly increases its power to help. Best of all: more women are writing and being published; finally, in the West at least, they—half of the race— are saying in their own voices what being human is like in their situations, from their points of view. This means that an entire vast experience—women's, still, and still sometimes slightingly, referred to as the 'domestic'—is at last, and perhaps not too late, being included in the making of human consciousness. And critically important though that material of their poetry is, more important and more hopeful still is that they are not bound to it, not confined within it, any subject is theirs, to be treated however they choose.

Saying the human, saying the whole irreducible, recalcitrant, fraught, contradictory energetic plurality of humankind, is a bid for a consciousness adequate to what we are and so, intrinsically, a demand for a politics that will help. The energy of poetry is itself hopeful. The stuff of it—the steadily truthful but not despairing contemplation of ourselves—is the necessary premise for survival. The agility of poetry, the challenges it issues to our imagination, is itself a resource that may help us change our lives. For if we don't wise up, imagine better, think differently, engage ourselves more fully, live altogether less narrowly, choose day by day to try to live in truth—in a word, if we don't revolt, we shan't survive. Thinkers in the twentieth and twenty-first centuries foretelling our end under the mechanisms we have ourselves created and no longer control, are legion. We have enslaved ourselves to principles, mechanisms, mindsets that will, if let, annihilate us and the good earth too. By revolt, I mean our self-emancipation, the freeing of ourselves from certain by now mortally dangerous ways of being human. Poetry—all the arts, but poetry is my particular concern—can help. It can help waken, enliven, and encourage us into demanding a politics more likely to keep us alive (and living in a livelier fashion) than what is offered or forced on us now. The insistent utopian faith of poetry is that we are capable of asking more of ourselves, we are not so beyond hope as it often seems. Utopian thinking these days—the impasse, the cul-de-sac, fears of a violent endgame—has perhaps a different relationship with the status quo than it once had. Erich Fromm said in 1976, 'The "utopian" goal is more realistic than the "realism" of today's leaders.'[24] If there are degrees of truth, that can't be less true now than it was then.

Notes

1. Friedrich Engels, in *Marx-Engels. Studien Ausgabe*, ed. Iring Fetscher, 4 vols. (Frankfurt: Fischer Verlag, 1982), II, 18. All further references to Marx and Engels are to this edition and follow the quotations in my text.

2. Daniel Dorling, *Injustice* (Bristol: Policy Press, 2011), 278–9.

3. Lawrence, *Selected Literary Criticism*, 105–6 and 108.

4. *Guardian* obituary, 19.12.2011.

5. Czesław Miłosz, *The Captive Mind* (London: Penguin, 2001), 151.

6. D. H. Lawrence, 'Introduction to "Memoirs of the Foreign Legion"', in *Phoenix II* (London: Heinemann, 1968), 357–8.

7. See also Robert Graves on his collections of poems after the First World War: 'They are coloured by the contemporary view of humanity as convalescent after a serious nervous break-down and resolved on a complete reorganization of its habits and ideas. It was easy to identify myself closely with convalescent and reconstructive humanity...My hope was to help the recovery of public health of mind, as well as my own, by the writing of "therapeutic" poems; and to increase their efficacy by a study of the nature of poetry "from subjective evidence"'—in *The Common Asphodel* (London: Hamish Hamilton, 1949), vii.

8. W. B. Yeats, *Essays and Introductions* (New York: Macmillan, 1961), 509.

9. *The Captive Mind*, 65. All translations of Miłosz are by Jane Zielonko.

10. Elizabeth David, *English Bread and Yeast Cookery* (London: Allen Lane, 1977), 391.

11. W. G. Hoskins, *The Making of the English Landscape* (London: Penguin, 1970), 247–8.

12. Hollis, *Now All Roads Lead to France*, 82.

13. In 'A Defence of Poetry', in *Shelley's Prose*, ed. David Lee Clark (London: Fourth Estate, 1988), 294.

14. D. H. Lawrence, in 'Morality and the Novel', *Selected Literary Criticism*, 109.

15. David Jones, *In Parenthesis* (London: Faber and Faber, 1975), 163.

16. Václav Havel, *Living in Truth* (London: Faber and Faber, 1989), 43, 12, 13.

17. Havel, *Living in Truth*, 85.

18. Nietzsche, *Werke*, I, 254.

19. In the section 'Eintritt' of his essay 'Winckelmann und sein Jahrhundert' (1805).

20. In 'On Love', *Shelley's Prose*, 171.

21. Novalis, *Schriften*, ed. Paul Kluckhohn and Richard Samuel, 5 vols. (Stuttgart: Kohlhammer, 1977–88), III, 447.

22. Edward Thomas, *Collected Poems*, edited by Edna Longley (Highgreen: Bloodaxe Books, 2008), 297.

23. Brecht, in the essay 'Bei Durchsicht meiner ersten Stücke' [On looking through my first plays], on the subject of *Baal*.

24. Erich Fromm, *To Have or to Be* (London and New York: Continuum, 1997), 163.

5

The Common Good

The readership

When John Clare was thirteen or so he borrowed a damaged copy of Thomson's *Seasons* for a few hours. The opening lines of 'Spring' made his heart 'twitter with joy'. He had to have a copy of his own. He persuaded his father, an illiterate agricultural labourer, to give him the necessary one shilling and sixpence, more than a day's wages, and walked the five or six miles to a bookseller in Stamford, found the shop closed (he had forgotten it was Sunday), walked home and next day walked there again, first paying a friend one penny to mind the horses that he, Clare, should have been minding and another penny to keep quiet about it. He got to Stamford by 6.30 in the morning and sat on the step till the shop opened. The bookseller let him have Thomson sixpence cheaper. Walking home, unable to wait, Clare climbed over the wall into the Marquis of Exeter's property, Burghley Park, and there, out of sight, he read.[1]

In the riots of 2011 in London, Salford, and other places, nobody, so far as I know, stole books. They stole trainers, jeans, MP3 players, plasma-screen televisions, smart phones, that sort of thing—not books. Why would you bother stealing books? If your hunger for poetry was as keen as the boy John Clare's you could feed it legally for much less of your own or your family's funds than it cost him in 1806. You could assemble a good collection from Oxfam for very little. Or read it on the Web for free. That is a happy thought in the state we are in: for next to nothing, this country's, this continent's, the whole wide world's poetry, can be yours.

There is no Frigate like a Book
To take us Lands away
Nor any Coursers like a Page
Of prancing Poetry –
This Traverse may the poorest take
Without oppress of Toll –
How frugal is the Chariot
That bears the Human soul.

And if what I've been claiming for poetry is true, if you were even half-persuaded of what I believe wholly to be the good of it, you'd have the makings of a revolt in you more purposeful and promising than looting. Anyone who can read, can read poetry. And anyone can be read to and get by heart and whisper or chant aloud thereafter a goodly stock of it. This, say:

By St Thomas Water
Where the river is thin
We looked for a jam-jar
To catch the quick fish in.
Through St Thomas Churchyard
Jessie and I ran
The day we took the jam-pot
Off the dead man.

Or this:

O westron wynde, when wilt thou blow,
The small raine down can raine?
Cryst, if my love were in my armes
And I in my bedde again!

Or this:

Morning and evening
Maids heard the goblins cry:
'Come buy our orchard fruits,
Come buy, come buy:
Apples and quinces,
Lemons and oranges,
Plump unpecked cherries,
Melons and raspberries,
Bloom-down-cheeked peaches,

Swart-headed mulberries,
Wild free-born cranberries...'[2]

Poetry is for everyone. I stand by that, it is the premise of this book. But I have to concede that, reading Derek Mahon lately, his *Selected Poems* of 1990, and Seamus Heaney, his *Human Chain*, 2010, I had the uneasy feeling that the ground they spring from and have thriven in and assume their readers share may be withdrawing and disintegrating under forces as irresistible as those working on the glaciers and the ice caps in the warming world.

Maybe this is nothing new? Certainly with Modernism came a strong sense that any unitary or even coherent culture that might be presupposed by author and reader was rapidly disintegrating or already had. Eliot's *The Waste Land* is in large measure, *entre deux guerres*, a montage of cultural bits and pieces. But then the very documents of that disintegration—the works of Eliot, Pound, Joyce, Freud—become themselves further fragments shored against the ruins and lodge in the culture which later educated writers and readers assume and feel they have in common. Has that also, the unsteady *terra firma* of a culture of iconic bits and pieces, disassembled now?

For the more confident and unitary transmissions, you have to go much further back: to that from Greece to Rome and from Greece and Rome into the Renaissance and the eighteenth century; and they were the concern, almost the property, of about the same percentage of the population then as nowadays holds most of the nation's wealth.

Brecht, reading and writing in exile in Finland, thought English literature wonderfully whole compared with German which, for all its beauties, has been a thing of interruptions, fits and starts. On 14 September 1940 he noted in his journal: 'I'm reading a controversy between Matthew Arnold and Newman on translating Homer. Again and again: what a literature the English have!' Then on 20 September he amplified the point:

Only this summer, reading more English, have I really understood what a national literature, and so a literature altogether, is. That great succession of generations in the literary world, their battles and communications, their innovations which are

corrections, a tradition that facilitates progress instead of hin-
dering it! The literary figures of three centuries seem to be
living all at the same time in a single city, they know one
another, they compete...

Brecht was in Finland because he and his Jewish wife Helene Weigel
would have been murdered had they not got out of Germany fast
when Hitler came to power. Hundreds of other writers, under the
same threat, did the same. Literature in the Third Reich was *gleich-
geschaltet* [co-ordinated] like everything else. The state fabricated a
national literature out of books that suited or could be made to suit;
and burned and banned the rest. In German schools and universi-
ties from 1933 to 1945 pupils and students were taught only the
literature, German or foreign, approved of by the Party; and they
were taught it very *partially*. During the war, under a controlled
economy, publishers had to be granted the necessary paper before
they could proceed to a publication. An effective form of censorship.
The state allowed paper for authors and projects they felt could
serve the ideology and its war. The Schiller *Nationalausgabe* and the
Hölderlin *Grosse Stuttgarter Ausgabe*, large and exemplary scholarly
editions, were begun during the war, as though they might help
build and affirm the Nazi nation, a most peculiar idea, riddled with
contradictions. On 3 June 1941 Hitler personally banned all further
performances of Schiller's *Wilhelm Tell* and removed it from the
school curriculum, and you can see why: it justifies the assassination
of a tyrant. Audiences regularly interrupted Act III of Schiller's *Don
Carlos* by loudly and long applauding the Marquis von Posa's pas-
sionate pleas for freedom of thought. And had they ever read him,
the ideologues must have realized that Hölderlin was even less fit for
their purposes than was his mentor Schiller. In 1941 Friedrich Beiss-
ner, a classical philologist and scholar of German, was transferred
from editing Schiller to editing Hölderlin. That was his war-work:
Hölderlin's poems. Adolf Beck, similarly qualified but then lying
badly wounded in a field hospital in the Ukraine, was brought home,
unfit for further active service, and set to work on Hölderlin's letters.
In 1943, the centenary of his death, the Hölderlin-Gesellschaft was
founded, patron Dr Josef Goebbels; the first volume of the *Grosse
Stuttgarter Ausgabe* was published (poems up to 1800); as was also a

special Field Edition (100,000 copies) of Hölderlin's work, and off
went the soldiers into a war already lost with that in their packs. In
September 1943 the *Landesbibliothek* in Stuttgart, Adolf Beck's work-
place, was bombed. He turned in next day and sat at his desk amid
rubble and broken glass, transcribing the letters, ordering the
archive. But then, as more bombs fell on Stuttgart, destroying stocks
of Volume 1, and as the Allies took Paris and moved up through
Italy and the Red Army advanced across Poland and the death
camps began to be opened, the work on Hölderlin shifted for safety
to Bebenhausen, a fairy-tale castle in a forest north of Tübingen.
There Beissner and Beck got on with their job, faithful to the texts,
never bending them, omitting nothing.

Until 1970 the Hölderlin Archive continued to be housed in
Bebenhausen. I worked there in the winter of 1968, walked out
through the forest to the castle in the snow, I was the only visitor,
the archivist was obliging. I saw the Nazi years, the documents and
photographs, the 1943 celebrations, the uniforms, the flags, the
swastikas, the salutes. And with that at my back, I began to learn
what I had come to learn: Hölderlin's poems, his letters, the life and
works.

In 1945 German readers and writers had to reconnect themselves
to their own interrupted tradition and to all that for twelve years
had been unavailable from abroad. Another severance began in
1948–9 with the founding of the Federal Republic of Germany and
of the German Democratic Republic, and worsened in 1961 with
the building of the Berlin Wall. Until 1989 (and beyond) the two
Germanies quarrelled over 'the inheritance'; that is to say, each
claimed to be the rightful inheritor of the national literature. A
national literature, a canon, even a syllabus, is a fraught affair.

What I said there about Germany and will say later about Václav
Havel's Czechoslavkia, has to do with the literature a public is
allowed to read, and how freely. But turning to the here and now,
to more open societies, I must ask what the readership is for a litera-
ture freely and cheaply available to all of its nation's people and, in
translation, to the peoples of many other nations worldwide. Series
such as Penguin Classics and OUP's World's Classics, assessing their
likely markets, have transformed themselves in recent years into
popular scholarly editions. That is, they acknowledge that to come

to, say, Petrarch, Camões, or Baudelaire, most British and American readers will need a translation and will be glad of a critical introduction, a chronology of the poet's life and times, suggestions for further reading and notes. I did about 120 explanatory notes for my translation of Goethe's *Faust, Part I* and more than 300 for *Part II*. In both parts the Bible is a ground of the writing and of our reading; in *Part II* it competes with a dozen Greek and Latin authors, chief among them Homer, Euripides, and Lucan. And both parts are threaded through with Shakespeare. Those three—Bible, Classics, Shakespeare—are the main intertextual constituents, but there are scores of others that Goethe in the fifty years of his writing at *Faust* incorporated more or less significantly. Using texts in that way does not, of course, mean being bound by them. Goethe, known in his day as 'the old heathen', was what the Germans call *bibelfest*: he knew his Bible inside out; and Bertolt Brecht, atheist and Marxist, when asked in an interview for a women's magazine which book had influenced him most, answered, 'Sie werden lachen: die Bibel' [You'll laugh: the Bible].[3] Brecht and Goethe do exactly what they please, which is to say exactly what their own projects need, with the lifted texts. Often the usage is parodistic, which readers will not appreciate unless the text being parodied is at *their* disposal, in *their* reading, too.

Derek Mahon is a cultured poet who expects his readers to be the same. He is a translator of Villon, Laforgue, Corbière, Nerval, Jaccottet, Guillevic, Horace, Ovid, Pasternak, Rilke, and others. To many of his poems he attaches an epigraph, Dante, Rimbaud, Voznesensky, the Bible, Beckett, Camus, Woody Allen, Shakespeare, Emily Brontë, Schubert, and Hsiang Ch'u being among his sources. Many titles of the poems are like points of orientation on a cultural map: 'Van Gogh in the Borinage', 'Poem beginning with a line by Cavafy', 'Brecht in Svendborg', 'Knut Hamsun in old age', 'Ovid in Tomis', 'Jean Rhys in Kettner's', for example. And a high number of the poems carrying these co-ordinates are addressed to friends, which suggests some community of writer and readers, a shared culture and understanding. Mahon is a serious poet, he writes clearly and very concretely, he has, I am certain, not the least wish to be inaccessible. The whole *Gestus* of his poems is that of a man speaking of things of common interest and expecting to be understood. His

'Beyond Howth Head'—the title alludes to Molly Bloom's lyrical saying Yes—is littered (or sown) with dozens of further allusions, and is addressed to a friend, Jeremy Lewis, who would doubtless pick most or all of them up. At least two-thirds of the poems in that Penguin selection are strewn with such allusions in this way. One of the shorter ones is 'Tractatus', addressed to friends Aidan and Alannah. It begins: '"The world is everything that is the case" / From the fly giving up in the coal-shed / To the Winged Victory of Samothrace.' The poem makes an offering, suited to the named persons and to any like them, simlilarly cultured, in the wider world. 'Tractatus' is a beautiful and effective poem. In his second stanza, citing another contributor to our culture, Mahon enlarges the world beyond 'everything that is the case':

> The world, though, is so much more –
> Everything that is the case imaginatively.
> Tacitus believed mariners could *hear*
> The sun sinking into the western sea;
> And who would question that titanic roar,
> The steam rising wherever the edge may be?

Learned, witty, and—most important—heading, as it finishes, into *terra incognita*. But will readers who haven't heard of Wittgenstein (the first proposition of his *Tractatus* being the first line of this poem) and Tacitus and have never seen the Winged Victory resist being enlarged?

Of course, Mahon's world is not coterminous and identical with that of his readers and certainly not with the world of 'culture altogether'. It is of his making, it serves him as poet, he discovers (invents) the truth about himself, about his situation, by using the map references of his saints and heroes in the culture he grew up in, was educated in and has extended and ordered for himself in later years. Still that world has a definable more general composition and character. We could say it is a mainly (not solely, not always) European, Francophile, secular and humane culture, centred in Ireland, steeped in the literature, history, and the *topoi* of Ireland. His immediate readership would indeed have access to it and feel at home in it. In 'A Disused Shed in Co. Wexford', that very specific locality is extended in the verses to touch on the 'lost people of Treblinka and

Pompeii', into the overwhelming natural disaster of AD 79 and into the horror perpetrated by humans upon humans in Poland, 1942–3, both mass burials belonging to the shared inheritance of Europe. Still that poem and all the cosmos of his poetry are his and of his making. The poems are an existential act by which he makes his own essence. Everybody inhabits a more or less self-made world. Striking in his particular case is how he binds and integrates himself into an order of figures, of exemplary instances, which are named and familiar. Really, it is a bid to belong, and he engages his readers, his like-minded friends, in that belonging too.

It may be that such presumption of a readership works more plausibly in Ireland—and also in Scotland and Wales?—than it would now in England or in the United Kingdom as a whole. The English self-identity is notably unsure, that of the UK still more unsure; which must affect a poet's sense of location and who he or she might honestly address in any public way, let alone speak for. And even the Irish presumption only rings true if, as in Mahon's poetry, it comes haunted with the fear of becoming unsustainable, implausible, ineffectual, even as a *bid* for a community and a readership, as a determined holding on. 'Beyond Howth Head' is riddled with anxieties on that score. And the plethora of binding allusions may themselves be the demonstration of their own ineffectuality in the face of so much abrasion and loss.

Heaney's *Human Chain* has much to do with necessary memory, the links that connect us and ensure our humanity. The book has a greater poignancy in that these are poems written by a man recovering his memory after a stroke, and several very honestly treat the suffering and struggle, 'as the memorable bottoms out / Into the irretrievable…' (p. 84). But the kinds of memory are concentric, or at least largely overlapping, circles: what the one man does not want to forget, and what the culture he has always lived in still holds and risks losing. Speaking of things others have put their faith in, he says, 'Mine for now I put / In steady-handedness maintained / In books against its vanishing.' And he lists such books: 'of Lismore. Kells. Armagh. / Of Lecan, its great Yellow Book.' Those are Ireland's books, but in circles around that particular centre they are anyone's who knows of them and knows we need them. And among books, for the reader of Heaney, is *Human Chain*, and many more by him and by other poets living and dead. Their books hold—against the loss of steady-handedness and faith.

I was quoting there from the sequence 'Hermit Songs', which are 'for' Helen Vendler, who wrote the best book I know on Shakespeare's Sonnets. Is poetry only possible in a hermitage? Is it offered out from there to friends who are themselves hermits? The hermitage presents itself as an option, and might even be inevitable, in a culture which, for all the poet's love, knowledge, and effort, won't hold together, can't be widely shared. Mahon in 'Beyond Howth Head', the poem most strewn with markers of a common culture, toys with the idea of swapping his 'forkful of the general mess / for hazelnuts and watercress', like one of the old hermits who withdrew 'from the world-circles people make / to a small island in a lake'. But that's not what he wants, except perhaps as an interlude, to be quiet, to concentrate, to listen and attend; like all makers of poems, he belongs in 'the world-circles' among the people who make them. Poets, Hölderlin wrote, are 'the tongues of the people' and are as such 'eager to be where / Living things move and breathe around us, glad, disposed / To all and trusting, how else / Should we sing to all their own god?'[4]

There is a peculiar poignancy in Hölderlin's understanding his function as a poet in that way. In truth, he was on the margins and scarcely read. Those lines are a part of the brave endeavour of all of his poetry actually to bring into existence the readers, and through them the community, that the poetry needs for its life. Several of his poems are addressed to particular people. These are the like-minded, chief among them Susette Gontard, who might be comrades in the wish and struggle to bring the necessary community into being. Many of the largest poems imagine as actual what they themselves are striving to create; and their characteristic dynamism, their wave-like rising and falling back, is the expression of that restless striving and its defeats. For Hölderlin is the most honest of poets. He imagines, he prepares, he works to achieve a state you would be proud and glad to live in; and woven into the very body of that oeuvre is the sad admission that such a state is not yet. Poem by poem he builds at the polis, and at the heart of it a Parthenon, a religious work of art; all the while knowing that the very premises of such a society are absent and that what he makes in a poem is only poetry, vital, beautiful, inspiring, and not enough. He addresses a readership that does not exist, writes to induce it into life, knowing that only through it will the Republic ever be made. Continually his poems make one appeal to the readers they do not yet have, 'O kommt! O macht es wahr!' [o come, o make it true!].[5] Is the main difference between him and us—between him and Mahon, Heaney, and any who honestly address in poetry the state we are in now—that in 1800 he believed he was building at the not-yet, the still-to-be-brought-into-being, and we now, after the millennium, feel that even what in the common cause has ever been achieved, is slipping, fraying, undoing, and the writers are drifting on smaller and smaller bits of terra firma, like creatures on the disintegrating ice?

At least, for the making of his cosmos Hölderlin went to a culture—the Classical—which was common ground for the small reading public in his day. What he made of it was eccentric, his own; but any readers present and willing to try, could have had access through familiar shared assumptions and images. But he was strange, and unread.

In the United Kingdom, particularly in England, we don't have and can't even honestly desire a unitary or coherent culture any more. In reality we never did have one, it was always class-bound, hierarchical, and mostly excluded women from among its makers. Now the disintegration (to use a pejorative term) or the variety (to view it cheerfully) is staggering. At my granddaughter's primary school in East Oxford you are greeted by the photographs of a selection of the children saying 'Welcome!' in speech-bubbles in thirty languages, among which are Yoruba, Polish, Albanian, Russian, Greek, Bemba, Shona, Tetum, Dhivehi, Tagalog, and Konkani. The list changes according to the number of migrants and asylum-seekers coming to stay or passing through. The motley thronging at twenty past three when the children are collected by their parents and grandparents is a joyous and wondrous spectacle. Every one of those languages is the voice of a culture, it has its own songs, poems, sacred and profane stories, many of which, away from home, will not survive.

For poetry one welcome development over the last couple of decades is the dying and final death of the Queen's English and with it RP. Some so-called small publishers, Bloodaxe chief among them, now have lists which closely represent the many and varied vernaculars of the United Kingdom. British English itself is, worldwide, only one variety of the language and by no means the most widely spoken. Linguisticians believe that before very long, as the English of the Indian subcontinent expands and develops, ours here will seem a local dialect containing its own even more local and peculiar strains. Worldwide, as languages, like species, die out or are exterminated, local counter-movements fight to retain or recover them, and very often for poetry. People, and poetry, have a strong natural wish to be rooted, to live and belong in a local habitation, a large constituting part of which is language. Poets want a language they can call their own, the better—the more finely, more truthfully, and exactly—to say what it feels like being human in their particular time and place. The language they arrive at will be their own version, their own dialect with its own intonation; and blessed are those who can draw on a native English for their own growth and sustenance. The English language, in its abundant dialects, is one thing no government can privatize and make us pay to use. And in that language there are thirteen hundred years of poetry.

It is the responsibility and privilege of poetry to say the human in all its variety. The United Kingdom, having so much, so many vernaculars, in so small a space, is a good home for poetry to thrive in and do what it does best: to say, to remember, to keep vital things alive.

Poetry is for everyone. Little by little, if they wish it, all readers can be inducted into the knowledge—the connectedness—that will make their reading more enjoyable and productive (even without such knowledge, poems can hit home). Here knowledge really is power. It is a means to the productive pleasure of poetry, it enlarges, refines, intensifies that pleasure, and so the good of it, in the life you live. And knowledge of the kind that helps with the cultural grounds of poetry has never been so accessible. The slow democratization of knowledge has in our day suddenly accelerated and is, at least in the matter of access, using the World Wide Web, now almost complete. You could find out about Wittgenstein, Tacitus, the Winged Victory of Samothrace and most other things alluded to in most poetry, free and in no time at all. True, it will only help, or will help much better, if you do it because you want to know, because you want to read better, get further, be more profoundly affected. And you need to be able to sift, assess, productively apply the knowledge you get. Knowledge as an acquisition is worth no more than any other thing you might acquire; knowledge put to living, converted into being, that is the turning point.

But for that turning point we need a culture, a social ecology, in which humane letters are respected and encouraged. Pushed out to the margins, rated lower than disciplines having a more calculable 'impact', pushed out there and disregarded, they will indeed become again what they once were, something for the few, the wealthy few, and that will be to the great impoverishment of the many.

Humane letters in war and peace

On 1 October 1801 a preliminary peace agreement between Britain and France was published. It excited in William Blake hopes as large as Hölderlin's in February of the same year when, with the signing of the Peace of Lunéville, hostilities halted in Continental Europe. Blake wrote to his friend John Flaxman: 'The Reign of Literature & the Arts Commences. Blessed are those who are found studious of Literature & Humane and polite accomplishments. Such have their lamps burning & such shall shine as the stars.'[6]

R. H. Tawney, badly wounded on the first day of the Somme (he lay all day and all night in no-man's-land), the following February published an article in the *TES* on what he hoped for English education and humane letters after the war. He wrote:

> The fundamental obstacle in the way of education in England is simple. It is that education is a spiritual activity, much of which is not commercially profitable, and that the prevailing temper of Englishmen is to regard as most important that which is commercially profitable, and as of only inferior importance that which is not. The task of those who believe in education is correspondingly simple. It is to induce a larger number of their country-men to believe, and, if they believe it themselves, to believe more intently, that spiritual activity is of primary importance and worth any sacrifice of material goods,

and that, in fostering such activity, education, if not the most powerful, is at least the most readily available agency.

He noted that some had begun to believe that education itself might be commercially profitable; but thought such grounds

> an insecure foundation for educational reform, because, if it is given for commercial motives, it will also be withdrawn for commercial motives, and because it is the nature of the mind to which such motives are of primary importance to take short views even of commercial profit, and to grudge the disinterested support of the pursuit of knowledge, the postponement of possessing to effort, of enjoyment to toil and thought, without which even material wealth cannot successfully be pursued.[7]

A decent education system for the many—the very few, as Tawney pointed out, already had one 'lavish even to excess'—was, like decent housing ('homes fit for heroes'), something which, during the war at least, the other ranks were felt to have earned.

In 2011, when the public funding of the arts in the UK was being discussed, Churchill was enlisted as an ally against the cuts. When asked, during the last war, why not give up the arts budget to the war effort, he replied: 'Then what are we fighting for?' At least, that is said to have been his reply. Some diligent sceptics have since trawled through his millions of printed words and found no record of any such utterance. Never mind. It's the idea that counts. Good for Churchill if he uttered it; and if he didn't, good for whoever ascribed it to him. In Germany, in even worse circumstances, the committee furthering the publication of Hölderlin and Schiller argued, against some opposition, that complete editions of these authors were *kriegswichtig* [important for the war effort]; and they cited as good examples in such matters the English, who, they said, took the long view, saw what such investment would one day bring.

Whilst these German scholars were arguing the case for poetry, their rulers were pursuing policies explicitly intended to eradicate the humane tradition out of which that poetry and much else that was good and beautiful had grown. In Wolfenbüttel, Lessing's town,

they set up a major execution centre; and on the Ettersberg,
overlooking Weimar—the place that because of Goethe, Schiller,
Herder, and others, gave its name to Germany's classicism, and
later became the place of its first and brief democracy—they built
Buchenwald. They meant it when they said they had come to oblit-
erate the very idea of *Humanität* [humanity, humanism, humane
letters]. Goethe walked and composed on the wooded slopes of the
Ettersberg. One oak tree there, on account of his particular love of
it, became known as the *Goethe Eiche*. The builders of Buchenwald
enclosed this tree behind the wire. Prisoners were hanged from it.
Then on 24 August 1944, during an American air raid, it went up
in flames, which pleased those inmates who knew the story that
when Goethe's oak perished so too would Germany.

At the age of sixteen, after only seven years in England, only
seven years speaking English, Michael Hamburger was looking for
a publisher for his Hölderlin translations. They came out three years
later, in 1943, the centenary year; by which time Hamburger, the
German Jew, was in British army uniform. The Poetry Society
invited him to come and talk on Hölderlin, and read from his trans-
lations. He declined. His Company Commander summoned him,
and ordered him to accept, for the honour of the regiment. He
agreed. But his nerve failed him, he hid in the audience and got two
friends to read and talk for him. That invitation and the occasion,
like the translation and the publication themselves, were an absurd
and beautiful act, against hatred and evil. Hamburger commented:
'If I had asked myself at the time why that war was worth fighting,
I should have said, because such absurdities are possible in Britain,
and there was nothing I wouldn't do to keep them possible.'[8]

Poems are bread on the waters, messages in bottles, they may
land anywhere. I found a copy of *Poems of Hölderlin* in Llangollen,
four or five years ago. Published by Nicholson & Watson, it has
nearly 100 pages of introduction, then 140 of poems, the German
facing Hamburger's English, page by page. Quite something, in the
middle of a war against the native land of poet and translator!

Louis Aragon's *Le Crève-Coeur* was first published in a small edition
in Vichy France and at once suppressed by the German authorities.
A copy came to Raymond Mortimer in England, like 'a present
from the moon or the banks of the Acheron', he said; and that same

year, 1942, the Curwen Press in Plaistow reissued it, and in the
following year Aragon's next book, *Les yeux d'Elsa* (got out of France
through Switzerland), in the series Horizon-La France Libre, at six
shillings each. Both volumes were smuggled back into occupied
France. Poems in both do address the war, defeat, the struggle—
'Les lilas et les roses', 'Tapisserie de la grande peur', 'La nuit de
Dunkerque', for example—but more, particularly in the second vol-
ume, are love poems, to the poet's wife. And *Le Crève-Coeur* is dedi-
cated to her: 'A Elsa, chaque battement de mon coeur'. Striking also
is that these two volumes published at the start and under the boots
of 'the thousand-year Reich' contain, split between them, Aragon's
lengthy and precise essay on how rhyme might be managed in mod-
ern French verse.

Paul Éluard's 'Liberté' begins

> Sur mes cahiers d'écolier
> Sur mon pupitre et les arbres
> Sur le sable sur la neige
> J'écris ton nom
>
> Sur toutes les pages lues
> Sur toutes les pages blanches
> Pierre sang papier ou cendre
> J'écris ton nom

[In my schoolboy exercise books / On my desk and on the trees /
On the sand and on the snow / I write your name / On all the
pages read / On all the white pages / Stone blood paper or ash /
I write your name]

And sustains that structure till the last of its 21 stanzas, which reads

> Et par le pouvoir d'un mot
> Je recommence ma vie
> Je suis né pour te connaître
> Pour te nommer
>
> Liberté.

[And by the power of a word / I start my life again / I was born to
know you / To name you / Freedom]

The poem is what it seems, a love poem, whose final word was,
originally, the name of Éluard's wife: Nusch. In 1942 he changed

the last word to 'Liberté', and in that form 150,000 copies of the poem were dropped by the RAF over occupied France. Not that he shifted his love to an abstraction. Rather, that abstraction, 'Freedom', is made variously concrete in the unchanged poem's listing of the scores of places where the lover writes the beloved's name. A kindred passion. And how should love flourish and be innocently self-delighting under the occupation (the unfreedom) of an ideology that would annihilate it?

An ecology

On 8 April 1975 Václav Havel wrote an open letter to Gustáv Husák, General Secretary of the Czechoslovak Communist Party. This letter was one of the grounds for his being detained two years later and charged with subversion of the state. In it he addressed the question of culture, its vital social function, the impoverishment of any society whose authorities act against it. Culture, he wrote, is 'the main instrument of *society's self-knowledge*'. He concedes that the suppression of even most of a nation's literary periodicals chiefly hurts only their (relatively few) subscribers. Life goes on without them. But then he moves to analyse the deeper damage done; and what he says would apply to such losses however occasioned. He describes the bad effects in organic terms. Each such closure is, he says,

> the liquidation of a particular organ of society's self-awareness and, hence, an interference, hard to describe in exact terms, in the complex system of circulation, exchange and conversion of nutrients that maintain life in that many-layered organism which is society today; a blow against the natural dynamic of the processes going on within that organism; a disturbance of the balanced interplay of all its various functions, an interplay reflecting the level of complexity reached by society's anatomy. And just as a chronic deficiency of a given vitamin (amounting in quantitative terms only to a negligible fraction of the human diet) can make a man ill, so, in the long run, the loss of a single periodical can cause the social organism much more damage than would appear at first sight.

The good effects of any cultural occurrence are not, in Havel's view, confined within its own perhaps very small circle. Everything in society being interconnected, all citizens are, however faintly, touched by the moments in which human self-awareness is advanced or deepened; and all lose when such moments are not allowed to happen. And even if it had no effect, the making of an illumination is of itself important, because it proves, it keeps alive, a possibility. It *might* have had an effect. In their very occurrence such moments fulfil 'a certain range of society's potentialities—either its creative powers, or simply its liberties'. The continual loss of them will be cumulative, and may in the end be impossible to make up. Perhaps, after a long absence of the proofs of cultural effect, there will not be people left who 'will still find the strength to light new fires of truth'; how should they, what will be their resources, 'once there has been such thorough wastage not only of the fuel, but of the *very feeling that it can be done*'?[9] There we are back with Shelley. The loss of the feeling that truth can be imagined, the extinction of the very memory of that ability, is personal and social death. In that state we are dead and buried.

Havel's image of society is that of the web of life. Cut one thread, the whole living organism is impaired. We know about loss. Even twenty years ago Edward O. Wilson estimated that 27,000 species go into—are dispatched into—extinction every year. And languages, one a fortnight. Perhaps half of our 7000 languages will be gone by 2100. Such a peculiar hallmark ours, this drive and drift into mass extinction. Best think of our culture—learning, the arts, humane letters—as a threatened ecology.

Literary magazines, small publishers of poetry and of poetry in translation do not get forcibly suppressed in the UK. If they break any law—incite hatred, for example—they can, quite properly, be prosecuted, and might cease. But whatever a passing government thinks of these makers and outlets of culture, it would not act to close them down. All the same, in 2011 when the Arts Council announced who it would and wouldn't fund, the lucky ones looked around and knew they had been weakened by the loss of unlucky colleagues nationwide. In the Arts, in that ecology, we really are all in it together. Yes, it's the economy, stupid. But the economy, the choices it allows, is itself only the workings of a politics, or at least of a mindset, very unlikely to value activities that do not make money or are not obviously useful. A publisher giving up, a local theatre closing, presented as a sad necessity, nobody's fault, is of a piece with the withdrawal of public funding from the humanities in higher education. Arts, humane letters, are things you are perfectly at liberty to pursue, at your own expense; but the public encouragement of them, the endorsement of their value, will lessen and lessen. Not directed to die, but certainly not encouraged to live. As the hostile mindset becomes ever more pervasive, we shall head, without coercion, without government violation of any laws, towards the state Havel feared and all should mortally fear: 'the loss of the very feeling' that humane letters are worthwhile.

T. S. Eliot thought 'the historical sense' nearly indispensable to anyone who wished to continue being a poet beyond their twenty-fifth year. And that sense 'involves a perception, not only of the pastness of the past, but of its presence'. Having it, a poet would write 'not merely with his own generation in his bones, but with a feeling that the whole of the literature of Europe from Homer and within it the whole of the literature of his own country has a simultaneous existence and composes a simultaneous order'. This wants amending—Eliot, like Auden, seems not to know that women write, and there are traditions other than the European—but the essential thought is very valuable. Past and present literature are a living entity, 'what happens when a new work of art is created is something that happens simultaneously to all the works of art which preceded it...' By the arrival of the new work 'the *whole* existing order must be, if ever so slightly, altered; and so the relations, proportions, values of each work of art toward the whole are readjusted'. An understanding of that simultaneity of past and present is essential for the *making* of the tradition into which the new writer enters. Tradition 'cannot be inherited, and if you want it you must obtain it by great labour'.[10] Eliot is speaking of the poet. I would widen the circle to include the reader and the whole of the potential readership too. The labour *is* great (and deeply enjoyable) for the poet; and willingness and application at least will be asked of the widening readership. But with that, to encourage the study, we need a habitat, a culture, in which such study is believed beyond any shadow of doubt to be worthwhile.

Thomas Hardy observed, 'It bridges over the years to think that Gray might have seen Wordsworth in his cradle, and Wordsworth might have seen me in mine.'[11] Robert Graves and his wife, cycling over Salisbury Plain in the late summer of 1920, made a diversion and visited Hardy. These connections matter.

Thou art a scholar...

Housman asks what it is in Milton's line 'Nymphs and shepherds, dance no more...' that can cause tears to start in the reader's eyes.[12] Another such line for me is that given to Marcellus when the ghost of Hamlet's father reappears: 'Thou art a scholar, speak to it, Horatio...' Why so affecting? In part it is the respect shown by the soldier to the scholar and so to the office of scholarship, and the faith that scholarship fits him to deal with this terrifying portent. The poignancy is rather increased than lessened by his actual inadequacy ('There are more things in heaven and earth, Horatio, / Than are dreamt of in your philosophy...' *Hamlet*, 1.1.45; 1.5.174–5). But for me, and perhaps for many of my generation and a similar upbringing, the line, so lovely in its tone and rhythm, is charged with the gifts I was given and with what I owe still in return. In my childhood, all children going to any local school were 'scholars'. At Whitsun, when the church schools and the Sunday schools paraded, it was called 'walking with the scholars'. There's respect in the word; and something else that now, thoroughly cognizant of the long failure and betrayal, I should call utopian, the longing that the word should mean what it says, that all in schooling should rejoice in the name of scholars. And Marcellus makes me face the loving ghosts of my mother and father who got my brother and me into schooling far beyond their own. So charged with piety the line strikes home.

I don't feel this to be a nostalgia. I feel it to be the necessary looking back to a place of reliable encouragement, for its deployment in the here and now. Scholars! 'O kommt! O macht es wahr!'

Poetry survives. Scraps of Sappho's verses are found on the rubbish heaps at Oxyrhyncus; Mandelstam died in the camps but his wife and friends had his poems by heart; Heine came through the flames (professors and their students threw him in), unharmed. Miklós Radnóti, force-marched from a prison camp in the autumn of

1944, was shot and buried in a mass grave. He had his last poems
on him in a notebook. Those poems were exhumed with his body
eighteen months later and in Hungarian and many foreign lan-
guages have circulated since. He wrote in classical metres and in
rhyming stanzas, he set the beauty of form and the long tradition of
verse against the hatred, hysteria, and dumb brutality he was at the
mercy of. The stained notebook was brought home to his wife,
many of the poems in it were addressed to her:

> Soundless worlds are listening somewhere deep
> In the earth; the silence roars in my ears and I keep
> On crying for help but from Serbia stunned by war
> No one can give me an answer and you are far
> Away. The sound of your voice becomes entwined
> With my dreams and, when I awake next day, I find
> Your words in my heart; I listen and meanwhile the sound
> Of tall, proud ferns, cool to the touch, murmurs all round.
>
> When I'll see you again, I can no longer promise – you
> Who once were as grave as the psalms, and as palpably true,
> As lovely as light and shade and to whom I could find
> My way back without eyes or ears – but now in my mind
> You stray through a troubled land and from somewhere deep
> Within it your flickering image is all I can keep
> A hold of.
>
> > (From 'Letter to my Wife', trans. Stephen Capus)[13]

Poetry, like love and the demand for happiness, is unkillable. Hav-
ing come through the worst tyrannies, the most annihilating ideolo-
gies, it will surely survive the unsatisfactory state we are in today.
But we want more for it than survival. In our 'rich and fruitful land',
in which there are, as in Blake's day, many things to be seen that
are by no means holy, we want for poetry something closer to vic-
tory than mere survival. On the arts altogether and on poetry in
particular rides a great energy demanding better for the brief lives
of human beings. Much works against that force for good, much
that reduces and demeans people, that hates and fears the desires
for a full humanity. Fundamentalisms of one stamp or another;
man-made and man-inflicted ideologies; and the helplessness and
hopelessness that the workings of these induce in a people told there

is no alternative. Poetry, which I don't conflate with but do closely ally to the bid for a fulfilled humanity, will survive in that hostile context and will answer back. But an ethos, an enveloping mindset hostile or even merely indifferent to humane letters must give poetry a bias towards the oppositional, warp it towards always being read and written in that way; which would lessen its power. That is why the defence of poetry entails the larger campaign for a humane habitat in which it may flourish to its heart's content, abundantly saying the human, and not just as an answering back against the inhumane, but also—why not?—in celebration of a society we are glad and proud of. Is that too much to ask? Too much or not, we have to demand it. We want more than mere survival, we want our due, our redress, lives fit to be looked at, and poetry will help, poetry at the heart of social life. We don't want poetry to be read by a dwindling few but by an increasing many. We want it commonplace, companionable, always there to be turned to, in our ordinary lives, customary and working wonders.

Notes

1. See Edward Storey, *A Right to Song: The Life of John Clare* (London: Methuen, 1982), 67.
2. Poets quoted: Emily Dickinson, Charles Causley ('By St Thomas Water'), Anon. sixteenth century (or earlier), Christina Rossetti ('Goblin Market').
3. *Die Dame*, October 1928, in its supplement. Brecht was interviewed shortly after the scandalous success of *The Threepenny Opera*.
4. Hölderlin, II, 66 and 62. I have brought together two versions of the same poem.
5. Hölderlin, II, 89—in the elegy 'Stutgard'.
6. Blake, *Complete Writings*, 810.
7. R. H. Tawney, *The Attack* (London: Allen & Unwin, 1953), 30 and 32.
8. Michael Hamburger, *A Mug's Game* (Manchester: Carcanet, 1973), 109.
9. Havel, *Living in Truth*, 16, 20–1, 22–3. Here and in Chapter 4 the translator of Havel is Paul Wilson.
10. 'Tradition and the Individual Talent', in *Selected Prose of T. S. Eliot*, 38–9.
11. Florence Emily Hardy, *The Life of Thomas Hardy* (London: Macmillan, 1972), 386.
12. Housman, *The Name and Nature of Poetry*, 46.
13. *Modern Poetry in Translation*, 3/13 (Spring, 2010), 151.

Further Reading

Neil Astley (ed.), *Staying Alive* (Newcastle: Bloodaxe Books, 2002); *Being Alive* (Newcastle: Bloodaxe Books, 2004); *Being Human* (Newcastle: Bloodaxe Books, 2011).

W. H. Auden, *The Dyer's Hand* (London: Faber and Faber, 1975).

Zygmunt Bauman, *Modernity and the Holocaust* (Oxford: Polity Press, 1995).

Samuel Taylor Coleridge, *Biographia Literaria* (London: Everyman, 1949).

David Constantine, *A Living Language* (Newcastle: Bloodaxe Books, 2004).

Danny Dorling, *Injustice* (Bristol: Policy Press, 2011).

Erich Fromm, *To Have or to Be?* (London and New York: Continuum, 1997).

Robert Graves, *Mammon and the Black Goddess* (London: Cassell, 1965); *Poetic Craft and Principle* (London: Cassell, 1967).

Václav Havel, *Living in Truth* (London: Faber and Faber, 1989).

Seamus Heaney, *The Redress of Poetry* (London: Faber and Faber, 1995).

Paul Hyland, *Getting into Poetry* (Newcastle: Bloodaxe Books, 1992).

Tony Judt, *Ill Fares the Land* (London: Allen Lane, 2010).

John Keats, *The Letters of John Keats*, ed. Robert Gittings (Oxford: Oxford University Press, 1970).

D. H. Lawrence, *Selected Literary Criticism*, ed. Anthony Beal (London: Mercury Books, 1961).

Czesław Miłosz, *The Captive Mind* (London: Penguin, 2001).

James Reeves, *Understanding Poetry* (London: Pan Books, 1965).

Peter Sansom, *Writing Poems* (Newcastle: Bloodaxe Books, 1994).

Index